60-MINUTE MUSEUM VISITS:
NEW YORK CITY

60-Minute Museum Visits: New York City

by
JoAnn Bright

Published by Quick View Publications, P.O. Box 4037, Mountain View, CA 94040.

Copyright © 1997, 1998 by JoAnn Bright.

Bright, JoAnn.
    60-Minute Museum Visits: New York City.

First Printing 1997
Second Printing 1998, revised.

Book and Cover Design: Jan & Martin Haseman, London Road Design

Compositors: Robert E. Bihlmayer, and Martin Haseman, London Road Design

Proofreader: Vicki Wilhite, London Road Design

Cover Photograph: The Statue of Liberty, Courtesy of the National Park Service.

Photos of museum exteriors and interiors are by JoAnn Bright.

Museum Floorplan Maps by Andy U'Ren, London Road Design

City Location Maps by David Lindroth, Inc., adapted from bases created for The New York City Convention and Visitors Bureau.

ISBN: 0-9650580-2-6

Publisher's Cataloging-in-Publication
Bright, JoAnn.

        60-minute museum visits : New York City / by JoAnn Bright
        — 2nd ed., rev.
        p. cm.
        Sixty-minute museum visits
        Includes index.
        "Self-guided tours of major museums, plus a directory of all
        museums and places of interest."
        Preassigned LCCN: 96-92158
        ISBN: 0-9650580-2-6

        1. Museums—New York (State)—New York—Guidebooks.
        2. New York (N.Y.)—Guidebooks. I. Title. II. Title:
        Sixty-minute museum visits

        AM13.N5B75 1998   069'.09747'1
                                           QB197-41614

For Ross

Acknowledgments

Thanks go to The American Museum of Natural History: Dr. George Harlow, Department of Earth and Planetary Sciences; Dr. Nancy B. Simmons, Department of Mammalogy. Metropolitan Museum of Art: Liz Markham, Public Relations; Dr. Dorothy Kellett, Department of European Paintings; John K. Howat, American Paintings and Sculpture; Jeannie Wienke. Brooklyn Museum: Barbara Gallati, American Paintings Collection; Jack Kennedy, Public Information. The Frick Collection: Susan Galassi. The Cloisters: Mary Shepard, Alexandra Givens. The Department of the Interior. Con Edison Energy Museum: Carol Green. Lefferts Homestead: Viviene Shaffer. New Museum of Contemporary Art: Katie Clifford. New York Historical Society: Stewart Desmond. Historic Richmond Town: Judith McMillen. China Institute of America: Willow Hai Chang. American Museum of the Moving Image: Graham Leggett. New York Transit Museum: Richard Madigan. New York Public Library: Liz Smith. American Academy of Arts and Letters: Virginia Dajani. Abigail Adams Smith Museum: Jane Covell. Museum of the City of New York: Marly Haye. Gracie Mansion: David Reese. The New York Convention and Visitors Bureau, Inc. Maps: David Lindroth, Inc.

My sincere appreciation to Martin and Jan Haseman of London Road Design for their creative book design and to W. D. "Zeke" Wigglesworth of the *San Jose Mercury News* for his editing and valuable insights into creating a travel guide. More thanks go to Ian Thonney for his diligence as a research assistant, and to all of the public information associates, museum directors, and curatorial associates who helped keep the information in this book on track.

Special thanks, and great affection, go to my children, Harry, Lisa, Trisha, and Marta, who cheered me on, and to Mirabai Bright-Thonney and her brother, Sam, both of whom arrived in the midst of this project and happily changed our lives.

Finally, and most especially, I want to thank my husband, Dr. Ross Bright, for his encouragement, for his support, and for his confidence in me.

Table of Contents

For You, the Reader

60-Minute Museum Visits: New York City serves three main purposes:

1. It suggests short tours which allow you to see key exhibits in large museums within a short period of time. The tours are especially designed to accomodate tourists on tight schedules.

2. It provides explanations of featured attractions to help you better understand and appreciate what you're seeing.

3. It provides an extensive directory that lists a multitude of smaller, lesser known museums located throughout New York City. These include art, science and history-house museums, children's museums, and museums that appeal to special interests such as fashion design, military themes, high tech, film, television, crafts, and more.

This book is written in the sincere belief that it will open your eyes to many exciting and interesting cultural experiences. I hope you will find pleasure in the places you visit, come upon some wonderful surprises, and return home treasuring them all.

How to Use this Book

■ Read the Table of Contents.

■ Take a close look at **Part I, 60-Minute Visits to Major Museums** which features the short tours of the largest and most popular museums. This will help you decide whether they offer the types of collections that interest you.

■ Browse through **Part II, The Directory.** Here you'll find an overview of 90 museums and historic houses (fourteen of these are new to this edition). These smaller museums are a joy to visit because they're usually not crowded, have excellent collections, and their exhibits are highly creative and informative.

■ Check out the information at the back of the book. The section titled **Types of Collections and Where to Find Them** has particular appeal for those with special interests and hobbies. **New Museum Listings** offers more places to visit and things to see and do around New York City. **Museum Tips** gives helpful advice on how to make your museum visits more fun and less tiring. **What's New: Updates** tells you about improvements and changes currently taking place in the major museums.

Part I:
60-Minute Visits to Major Museums

The American Museum of Natural History

Address:
Central Park West at 79th Street
(Manhattan, Upper West Side)
New York, New York 10024-5192
(212) 769-5100 recorded information

Hours:
Open: Sunday–Thursday 10–5:45;
Friday–Saturday 10–8:45
Closed: Museum and Hayden
Planetarium closed
Thanksgiving and Christmas

Entry Fees:
Suggested donation

Type:
Science, natural history,
and planetarium

Transportation:
Subway: B or C to 81st Street
Bus: M7, M10, or M11
to 79th Street; on-site
parking available

Museum Shop:
Yes. Several located throughout the
building. All are excellent and have
unique gift items, clothing, jewelry,
games, models, posters, toys, and
crafts from around the world.

Restaurant:
Yes. Garden Cafe serves lunch and
dinner; Diner Saurus serves light meals,
snacks, salads; Whale's Lair provides
cocktails and snacks, and is open
weekends and holidays.

Disabled Access:
Yes

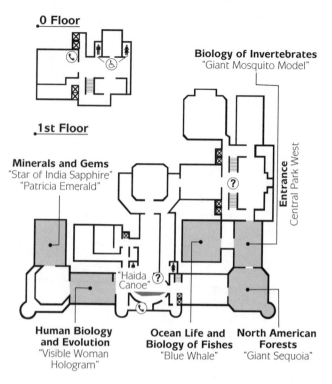

0 Floor

1st Floor

Biology of Invertebrates
"Giant Mosquito Model"

Minerals and Gems
"Star of India Sapphire"
"Patricia Emerald"

Entrance
Central Park West

"Haida Canoe"

**Human Biology
and Evolution**
"Visible Woman
Hologram"

**Ocean Life and
Biology of Fishes**
"Blue Whale"

**North American
Forests**
"Giant Sequoia"

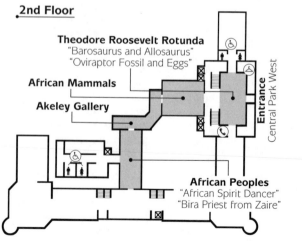

2nd Floor

Theodore Roosevelt Rotunda
"Barosaurus and Allosaurus"
"Oviraptor Fossil and Eggs"

African Mammals

Akeley Gallery

Entrance
Central Park West

African Peoples
"African Spirit Dancer"
"Bira Priest from Zaire"

3rd Floor

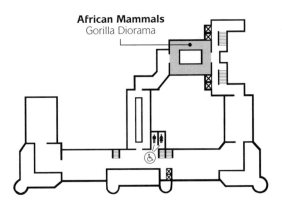

African Mammals
Gorilla Diorama

4th Floor

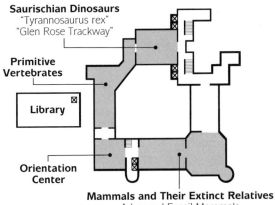

Saurischian Dinosaurs
"Tyrannosaurus rex"
"Glen Rose Trackway"

**Primitive
Vertebrates**

Library

**Orientation
Center**

Mammals and Their Extinct Relatives
Advanced Fossil Mammals
"Evolution of Horses"
"Warren Mastodon"

*This floor plan highlights only the areas included in the suggested tours.
A detailed floor plan of the museum is available at the Information Desk.*

What to Expect

This much-loved institution ranks as one of the largest natural history museums in the world with more than 30 million artifacts and specimens in its collection. What's even more amazing is that despite its massive size and endless galleries, less than two percent of the entire collection is actually on display!

One of the reasons for the American Museum of Natural History's success is that there is something to interest people of all ages. In more than 40 halls and galleries you can see dioramas with animals in natural settings, experience life on the African plains, learn about the human body, be wowed by dinosaurs or giant whales, see dazzling gems, partake in numerous educational programs, see special exhibitions, and just plain have fun.

Some of the major attractions you'll definitely want to see are the new dinosaur galleries featuring *Tyrannosaurus rex* and the Hall of African Mammals with eight adult Indian elephants and numerous dioramas that feature gorillas, lions, tigers, and even a rhino or two. The Hall of North American Forests with its gigantic slice of the Mark Twain Tree is a popular favorite, as is the fabulous Star of India sapphire, the largest in the world. Or you can just take time to view a movie at the IMAX Theater or visit the colossal 94-foot model of a female blue whale in the Hall of Ocean Life and the Biology of Fishes. Children will love the educational games in the Discovery Room and everybody enjoys watching live programs featuring music, dance, and crafts in the Frederick H. Leonhardt People Center. Be sure to call ahead for information about special events and exhibitions.

With so much to see and do, you'll want to return again and again.

Suggested 60-Minute Tour

Two tours are suggested.

Tour 1: *Go on a more general tour that leads to various sites and objects of interest within the museum.*

Tour 2: *Spend an hour in the newly redesigned and renovated Dinosaur Halls on the fourth floor.*

More time will be necessary if you want to see one of the Museum's excellent movies in the IMAX Theater or visit the Hayden Planetarium.

Remember to get a complimentary museum floor plan.

Highlights

TOUR 1: Begin on the first floor in the Hall of Minerals and Gems.

**Star of India Sapphire
Location: Hall of Minerals and Gems (First Floor)**

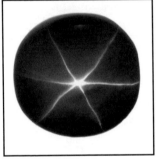

photo by Craig Chesek

The Star of India, one of the most renowned objects in the Museum's collections, is the largest and most famous sapphire in the world. It weighs in at 563 carats and was discovered some 300 years ago in Sri Lanka.

> *In 1964, one of the most notorious burglaries of this century occurred when Jack Murphy, also known as "Murph the Surf," masterminded the theft of the Star of India Sapphire from the museum. Fortunately the burglars were caught in several days and the gem was returned to the museum eight weeks later.*

Tiny needles of the mineral rutile give the gem the appearance of a milky white star in its center. The gem's domed (cabochon) shape also enhances the appearance of the star as incoming light reflects off its surface. This effect is known as *asterism*, and, along with richness of color, is one of the characteristics that makes star sapphires so precious.

**The Patricia Emerald
Location: Hall of Minerals and Gems (First Floor)**

This spectacular emerald crystal, discovered in the Colombian Andes at the Chivor mines in 1920, weighs 632 carats, making it one of the largest in the world. It has twelve sides, twice that of most emerald crystals, and is one of the few gem-quality stones that has been left uncut. The small flaws you see are found in all emeralds, making them less durable and transparent than other precious gems. Although emeralds have been mined in the United States, Egypt, and the Russian Ural Mountains, today the best ones still come from Colombia.

> **Emeralds and superstition**
> *Many folktales existed about the powers of emeralds. According to common beliefs during the Medieval era, they could ward off evil spirits, cure dysentery and epilepsy, reduce eyestrain, and make childbirth easier.*

Giant Sequoia
(The Mark Twain Tree)
Location: Hall of North American Forests (First Floor)

This representative slice from a giant sequoia was taken from a tree that was felled by loggers in 1891. It once stood over 300 feet high, the equivalent of a 30-story building, and is estimated to be 1,342 years old. Giant sequoias owe their longevity to several factors: its unusually thick bark is fire-resistant and the tree also contains a natural wood preservative that is very resistant to fire and disease.

The sequoia slab demonstrates how the age of a tree can be determined using a system of counting its concentric growth rings outward from its center. Each ring represents one year's growth. Markers have been placed at different intervals to denote significant events that occurred in world history during the tree's lifetime.

The finest specimens of living giant sequoias, many much older than the one represented here, are in greatest concentration at Kings Canyon and Sequoia National Parks in California. These giants are now considered national treasures, and it is illegal to cut them down.

Note: Temporary change for this exhibit. See page 171.

Visible Woman Hologram
Location: Hall of Human Biology and Evolution (First Floor)

The Visible Woman Hologram is an adaptation from an earlier version that was displayed in the Hall of the Human Biology of Man, now the Hall of Human Biology and Evolution. Layers from the earlier plastic (and static) form were taken apart, holographed, then reassembled to create separate images of the internal organs. This new interactive display now allows us to view the female figure in its entirety from the inside of the body to the outer layers. Stand to the right, in front of the hologram, and you'll see her skeleton; move farther to the left and her internal organs appear—lungs, stomach, intestines, glands, and so on. Keep moving left, and the arteries, veins, nerves, flesh, and hair appear.

Giant Mosquito Model
Location: Hall of the Biology of Invertebrates (First Floor)

Don't miss this outsized model of an *Anopheles* mosquito, with hairs made of brass and body made of wax. A threat of a malaria outbreak in the New York City area was the inspiration for making this realistic replica. The museum originally put the mosquito on display in 1917 to educate the public about how malaria is transmitted from insect to human. Oddly, this is a model of a male mosquito, which does not carry the disease. Only female insects bite and transmit malaria to humans. The model is 75 times life size.

Note: Temporary change for this exhibit. See page 171.

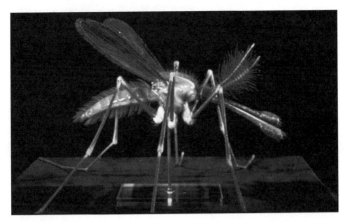

Giant Mosquito Model

Great Blue Whale
Location: Hall of Ocean Life
and the Biology of Fishes
(First Floor)

This 94-foot-long fiberglass replica of a female blue whale is one of the most popular displays in the museum. It is modeled from a whale caught in 1925 off the coast of South Georgia Island near Tierra del Fuego, at the tip of South America.

Blue whales, the largest mammals on our planet, can grow to be 110 feet long and weigh more than 100 tons! They consume huge quantities of krill each day, straining the small shrimp-like animals through the baleen, long bristle-like plates that hang from their upper jaws.

Blue Whale

Whale blubber, source of an oil burned in lamps, was much sought after during the late 19th and early 20th centuries. Because the blue whale was the largest source of this commodity, it was hunted almost to extinction. Today there is a ban on the hunting of the blue whale and its population is now estimated to be 10,000 to 12,000.

Haida Canoe
Location: Hall of the Northwest Coast Indians (First Floor)

This 63-foot-long canoe was hand-crafted by the Haida Indians of the Pacific Northwest in 1878. This sea-worthy boat was carved from a single cedar tree trunk, originally three feet in diameter; the hull was then widened to eight-and-one-half feet by stretching the sides after softening it with boiling water. A carved wolf and paintings of a killer whale were then added as decorative elements to its exterior. A canoe this size was used for war, for trade, and for traveling to ceremonial events.

The display, which was created in 1910 by George T. Emmons who explored the Pacific Northwest area for the Museum, is set up as though Indians are arriving at a potlatch, with slaves manning the canoe.

✳ **Fossil of _Oviraptor_**
Dinosaur with Eggs
Location: Theodore Roosevelt Memorial Rotunda (Second Floor)

Great excitement has been created by the recent discovery of this fossilized 9-foot-long _Oviraptor_ dinosaur sitting in a protective position over a clutch of its eggs. This important specimen

was unearthed by a group of paleon-tologists from the American Museum of Natural History in Mongolia's Gobi Desert in 1993. It has been sug-gested that the nest was buried by a sandstorm 72 million years ago.

The position in which the dinosaur and eggs were found point for the first time to a definite link in the behavior patterns of dinosaurs and birds. The 72-million-year-old fossil remains show the dinosaur skeleton in a protective sitting posi-tion with its back legs tucked up under itself, resembling the posture assumed by modern chickens. Its arms appear to encircle the eggs in a protective gesture, as though guard-ing them from predators. The eggs, between 15 and 22 of them, are in a circle with the blunt ends pointing inward, in similar fashion to the way modern birds arrange their eggs.

Oviraptor (a Latin term meaning "egg-thief") walked on two legs, and was a meat-eater and a member of the same theropod group as _Tyran-nosaurus rex._

Note: Temporary change for this exhibit. See page 171.

Interior, Theodore Roosevelt Rotunda

Barosaurus and *Allosaurus*
Location: Theodore Roosevelt Memorial Rotunda (Second Floor)

If you were alive 140 million years ago, no doubt you would have run across *Barosaurus,* a giant plant-eating dinosaur. This enormous beast, rising 50 feet into the air, is dramatically presented in combat, trying to protect its baby from an attack. No one is certain if *Barosaurus* could really rear up on its hind legs, but the hypothetical scene is very effective. The dinosaurs' skeletons are actually fiberglass casts made from real bones.

Fossil remains of *Barosaurus* have been found on two continents—Africa and the western United States—and are extremely rare.

African Spirit Dancer Snail Shell Cape
Location: African Peoples Galleries (Second Floor)

Tricks, jokes, disappearing acts, and other kinds of frivolity are what you might expect of this Marikoto figure wearing the elaborate cape made entirely of snail shells. As he moves around, the shells make rattling noises.

Marikoto plays an important role in the Nigerian Yoruba Egungun cult's spiritual ceremonies. As shown in this display, he takes on the characteristics of an entertainer. Anthropologists have recently broadened their interpretation of the part played by Marikoto, whom they originally believed was an ancestral figure whose sole function was to bestow blessings on the Yoruba people during religious ceremonies.

Bira Priest from Zaire
Location: African Peoples Galleries (Second Floor)

photo by Else Sackler

Almost adjacent to the African Spirit Dancer is the haunting image of the Bira Priest, whose body decorations represent both bird and beast. White circles around his eyes, and lines along the nose and mouth define his facial features. His entire upper body is covered with white star-like markings representing leopard spots. His strong dark arms have wrappings of raffia to symbolize a mythical bird. Priests who assume body decorations of the Spirit Dancer conduct ceremonies in which boys pass from childhood to manhood.

Akeley Memorial Hall of African Mammals (Second and Third Floors)

This hall is named for Carl Akeley, an explorer and taxidermist who led many expeditions to South Africa to collect the specimens seen here.

*Akeley was an innovative taxidermist who was the first to build interior armature to give each animal a more life-like appearance. He used metal, wood, wire, and bones to create the bodies, and modeling clay to define muscles and blood vessels. Over this the skin was drawn, resulting in a very realistic model of each animal. One of the most interesting displays is the **gorilla diorama**. The place in Africa where Carl Akeley is buried is depicted in the background to the right.*

You'll want to browse among the twenty-eight dioramas that make up this two-floor gallery. Each depicts animal and plant life from a variety of habitats in Africa.

∗ Gorilla Diorama
Location: Akeley Hall (Third Floor)

Gorillas belong to the order of primates and to the *Pongidae* family (great apes) which also includes the chimpanzee and orangutan. They are closely related to monkeys and humans.

The gorilla is the largest of this family, with males sometimes reaching six feet in height and weighing 300 to 400 pounds. They're so large, in fact, it's difficult for them to live in trees as do their smaller cousins. They remain erect when they walk, but use all four limbs with the knuckles of the hands to support the upper body.

Gorillas live in family groups, comprised of several females, offspring, and a single male as its leader. As the male matures, the hair on his back turns silver—thus the name "silverback" to designate the adult male.

Their size and appearance have led people to believe they're mean and aggressive. Quite the contrary. Gorillas live peaceably, interact well with other groups, and when conflicts arise, the males will often beat their chests to express their agitation rather than engage in direct physical assault.

TOUR 2: Begin on the fourth floor in the Dinosaur Halls.

Visitors should spend at least 60 minutes visiting this area of the museum. First go to the Orientation Center for background information before proceeding through the galleries. A good way to begin is to visit the Hall of Vertebrate Origins to see fossils of fish, turtles, marine reptiles, lizards, crocodiles, and the flying *Pterosaurus.*

Tyrannosaurus rex
Location: Hall of the Saurischian Dinosaurs

Wouldn't it be astonishing to come upon this gargantuan beast in the open spaces of Montana today? This is where the *Tyrannosaurus* remains were found during two separate excursions made by Museum paleontologist Barnum Brown in 1902 and 1908.

With some guidance from professionals in the field of paleontology, along with skilled museum preparators, two *Tyrannosaurus* specimens

Organization of the Dinosaur Halls

The fourth floor is arranged in a continuous loop of galleries which display the world's finest collection of vertebrate fossils. The layout is brilliantly conceived as a large evolutionary tree. As you walk along the main pathway, or "tree trunk," you may stop at a "branch" which represents new evolutionary features. Information signs at these junctures point out features such as the hole in the center of the hip socket, a characteristic shared by birds and dinosaurs that suggests a link between the two. Move farther toward smaller branching points and enter alcoves which point out groups of closely related dinosaurs with similar features such as hadrosaurs and sauropodomorphs. Each alcove has an information station with general information about the group. There is also an interactive computer designed by the Museum's curators to help visitors learn about new evolutionary features that evolved within each group. The advantage of this approach is that the visitor can understand the full scope of development of a group of dinosaurs from the earliest to the latest in one particular area.

Colored labels highlight information that addresses the most frequently asked questions designed for families with young children. There are also more advanced scientific labels that point out the best specimens and the most important scientific conclusions. In the alcoves you will find detailed technical scientific information on the evolutionary significance of each group.

have been cleverly combined to make this one spectacular display. Most of the bones are real and fossilized, not plaster molds.

Often referred to as *Tyrannosaurus rex*, this largest of all the dinosaurs is about 65 million years old and was a meat-eating beast. *Tyrannosaurus* may have weighed as much as eight tons, with a huge four-foot jaw lined with rows of six-inch-long flesh-tearing teeth. Short forearms, with two fingers on each hand, made it impossible to grasp food or reach the giant mouth. Their precise function, therefore, is not well understood. Enormous hind legs, up to ten feet long, held up the massive weight. The backbone was held horizontal to the ground so that the head and chest were counterbalanced by the long tail when the animal walked or ran.

Two theories prevail concerning the way in which *Tyrannosaurus* gathered food: one suggestion is that it stalked its prey, while another possibility is that it lived by scavenging.

The Glen Rose Trackway
Location: Hall of the
Saurischian Dinosaurs

These 107-million-year-old dinosaur footprints were unearthed by Roland T. Bird, a distinguished paleontologist who was in Texas on a dinosaur fossil-seeking expedition for the American Museum of Natural History in 1938. The tracks were discovered in an area of the Paluxy River, near Glen Rose, Texas, and they're important because they help scientists understand how dinosaurs stood and moved. The smaller impressions of the three-toed therapod, a meat-eating dinosaur, show how it walked on its two hind feet. The larger footprints are believed to be those of a plant-eating sauropod dinosaur, like *Apatosaurus*, whose feet measured one yard in length and three-quarters of a yard in width.

Tyrannosaurus rex

photo by Ben Blackwell, Denis Finnin

**Warren Mastodon
Location: Advanced
Fossil Mammals**

This giant elephantine creature lived during the Pleistocene epoch, and is a close relative of living elephants with its large skull, curving tusks, and its well-developed trunk. It was smaller than today's elephant and was known to roam North America.

The Warren mastodon is named for John Warren, a Harvard anatomy professor who owned and wrote about its remains and even displayed it in a museum in Boston. The Warren mastodon was discovered in 1845 by a crew digging for peat fuel in Newburgh, New York. It is believed to have died 11,000 years ago and was found in a standing position with head thrown back suggesting it was gasping for air. It's one of the best-preserved specimens of its kind anywhere, and all of the bones are original.

> **It's a fact:** The term mastodon is derived from a Greek word meaning "breast" and refers to the shape of the mammal's teeth which are formed like cone-shaped cusps. When viewed in profile, they resemble a woman's breasts.

**Evolution of Horses
Location: Hall of Mammals
and Their Extinct Relatives**

The Museum's collection of fossilized horses is the largest of its kind in the world. The display represents two approaches to the evolution of the horse. You'll notice that the fossil horses in the front of the case (from left to right) represent the evolutionary process as a progression along a single pathway, with the animals steadily growing larger and having fewer toes and larger teeth. This approach, until recently, was the most widely held view of their evolution.

Warren Mastodon   *photo by Scott Frances*

The more recent scientific view of the evolution of the horse is represented in the back row of skeletons, using a method of analysis called *cladistics*. This more complicated method groups organisms by shared specialized characteristics: each time a new evolutionary feature appears, a new branch grows on the evolutionary tree, comprising organisms that have both the old and the new characteristics. You'll notice that the later horses, *Callipus* (#46), for example, were actually smaller than the earlier ones, such as *Neohipparion* (#40), and still had three toes.

The Hayden Planetarium

The Hayden Planetarium is part of the American Museum of Natural History and serves as its department of astronomy. Main Entrance: 81st Street between Columbus Avenue and Central Park West. An additional entry fee is required.

Note: The Planetarium will close for renovations in March 1997.

All ages enjoy this facility which serves as both an educational and entertainment center that focuses on astronomical phenomena. Over 30 million people have visited the planetarium to see its special exhibitions and partake in numerous activities. **Highlights** include the **Sky Theater,** which is one of the largest sky theaters in the world (650-person capacity), and has an enormous 49-foot dome onto which a Zeiss Model VI Star Projector casts images of the universe. Lasers and discs provide stunning special effects including whooshing asteroids, rockets blasting from launch pads, shooting stars, and rock music, to the delight of teenagers. Cosmic laser light shows are featured on Friday and Saturday nights. Call (212) 769-5900 for information. See the 14-ton **Willamette meteorite,** the largest meteorite found in America, the **Bliss Collection**'s antique astronomical instruments and the **Black Light Gallery** with murals that glow in the dark. In the **Guggenheim Space Theater** there are 22 screens surrounding you for exciting slide presentations that serve as a prelude to the Sky Show. Also featured is a huge model of the solar system on the ceiling. **The Hall of the Sun** offers an innovative and participatory approach to sun-related subjects, including the sun's effect on climate, weather, agriculture, eclipses, rainbows, sunsets, time, and energy. **Astronomia** is an exhibition that is great for the history buff who enjoys seeing antique astronomical instruments and fanciful inventions, and loves discovering interesting facts and fiction related to astronomical topics past and present. **Your Weight in Other Worlds** is one of the Planetarium's most popular places to visit. You can use five different scales that will tell you what your weight is on Venus, Mars, Jupiter, the moon, and the sun. Preschoolers will enjoy the **"Wonderful Sky Show"** which features *Sesame Street* characters, who, with a host, interact through conversation and song to explain the wonders of the day and night sky.

"Robots in Space," featuring R2D2 and C-3PO for children 7–12, is so popular that you should reserve well in advance. It is shown on selected Saturdays and advance tickets are required. Call (212) 769-5900 for information. Adult courses on a variety of astronomical topics are offered evenings and weekends.

The Hayden Planetarium houses the **Richard S. Perkins Library** *(free, by appointment only) which has every imaginable book written on astronomy, earth and space science, aeronautics and astronautics, NASA reports, and periodicals. Students, academicians, the media, writers, and artists find this a valuable resource.*

Illustrations

p. 2: American Museum of Natural History, exterior

p. 7: Star of India Sapphire. 2A22941. Photo: Craig Chesek. Courtesy Department Library Services, American Museum of Natural History.

p. 9: (top) Malaria Mosquito Model. K4747. Courtesy Department Library Services, American Museum of Natural History.

p. 9: (bottom) Blue Whale. 2141. Courtesy Department Library Services, American Museum of Natural History.

p. 10: Interior, Theodore Roosevelt Rotunda

p. 11: Bira Priest from Zaire. NEH2453. Photo: Else Sackler. Courtesy Department Library Services, American Museum of Natural History.

p. 14: Tyrannosaurus rex. 2A22931. Photo: Ben Blackwell, Denis Finnin. Courtesy Department Library Services, American Museum of Natural History.

p. 15: Warren Mastodon. 2A22940. Photo: Scott Frances. Courtesy Department Library Services, American Museum of Natural History.

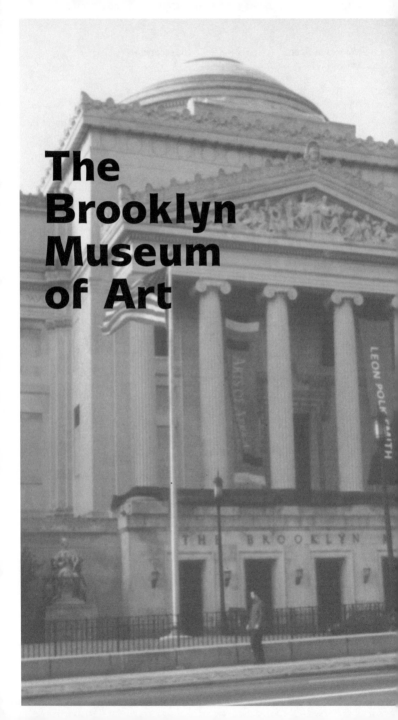

The
Brooklyn
Museum
of Art

Address:
200 Eastern Parkway
(Prospect Heights)
Brooklyn, New York 11238
(718) 638-5000

Hours:
Open: Wednesday–Sunday 10–5
Closed: Monday, Tuesday,
Thanksgiving, Christmas,
New Year's Day

Entry Fees:
Yes. Contribution.
Children under 12 free.

Type:
Art

Transportation:
Subway: 2 or 3 line to Eastern
Parkway/Brooklyn Museum
Bus: From Brooklyn: B71 in front
of Museum; B41 and B69
at Grand Army Plaza; B48 at
Franklin Avenue and Eastern
Parkway

Museum Shop:
Yes

Restaurant:
Yes

Disabled Access:
Yes; wheelchairs available
upon request at entrances

1st Floor

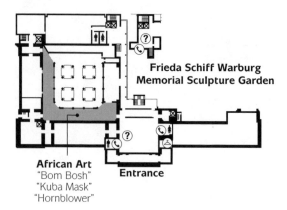

**Frieda Schiff Warburg
Memorial Sculpture Garden**

African Art
"Bom Bosh"
"Kuba Mask"
"Hornblower"

Entrance

2nd Floor

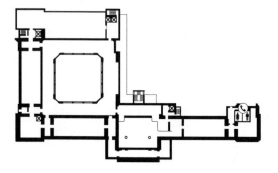

3rd Floor

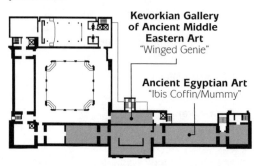

**Kevorkian Gallery
of Ancient Middle
Eastern Art**
"Winged Genie"

Ancient Egyptian Art
"Ibis Coffin/Mummy"

4th Floor

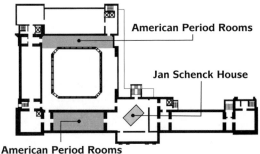

American Period Rooms

Jan Schenck House

American Period Rooms
"The Cupola House"
"Moorish Smoking Room"

5th Floor

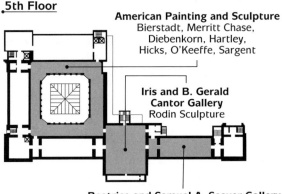

American Painting and Sculpture
Bierstadt, Merritt Chase,
Diebenkorn, Hartley,
Hicks, O'Keeffe, Sargent

**Iris and B. Gerald
Cantor Gallery**
Rodin Sculpture

Beatrice and Samuel A. Seaver Gallery
Diebenkorn, "Ocean Park"
Smith, "The Hero"

This floor plan highlights only the areas included in the suggested tour.
A detailed floor plan of the museum is available at the Information Desk.

What to Expect

Art lovers couldn't ask for a better place to visit than the venerable Brooklyn Museum. It ranks as the seventh largest museum in the nation and has in its collections over 1 million works of fine art, textiles, decorative arts, and objects of ethnographic interest.

The Egyptian collection in the newly renovated West Wing showcases such treasures as ancient sculptures of Egyptian royalty, sacred cats, dogs, mummies in elaborately decorated cases, wall reliefs, pottery, tools, and jewelry.

The American paintings collection is particularly strong, and spans the time between the Colonial period and World War II, with works by John Singleton Copley, John Singer Sargent, Edward Hicks, Georgia O'Keeffe, Marsden Hartley, Winslow Homer, and Thomas Eakins. European paintings and sculpture range from the Old Masters to important 19th-century works by Monet, Cassatt, Degas, Pissarro, and other French Impressionists. In the Iris and B. Gerald Cantor Gallery you'll find the best of Rodin's sculpture, including a memorable full-sized likeness of *Balzac*, and the heroic *Burghers of Calais*.

The decorative arts collection is also a great strength of the museum, with 28 American period rooms, dating from 1675 to 1928, making it one of the largest collections of its kind in the world. Crowd-pleasers include the exotic Moorish Smoking Room, taken from John D. Rockefeller's New York City mansion on 54th Street, and the reconstructed Dutch-American Schenck House.

Step outdoors to visit the charming Frieda Schiff Warburg Sculpture Garden, filled with 19th- and 20th-century architectural ornaments saved from New York City landmark structures. Among the gargoyles, lions, scrolls and theatrical masks cast in cement and terra cotta, you'll come upon a lamppost from Steeplechase Park, once an attraction on Coney Island.

Just adjacent to the museum is the famous Brooklyn Botanic Garden, a 53-acre park filled with specimen plants and trees. A visit to the museum's excellent cafe and giftshops will round out an interlude that will prove memorable for people of all ages and interests.

Special Information

- **Gallery talks daily.** The Grand Lobby. Check for times.

- **Changing exhibitions** feature contemporary artists and trends in contemporary art.

- **Arty Facts:** Saturday and Sunday 11 A.M. and 2 P.M. for children ages 4–7 with an adult. Combines gallery visits and art-making projects designed to bring art in a museum setting to life.

- **School Programs:** A wide variety of planned activities is offered through the education department. By special arrangement. Call (718) 638-5000 extension 221.

- **Museum Shop and artSmart Children's Shop:** The Brooklyn Museum has one of the best museum shops anywhere. Its unique items reflect the museum's permanent collection including handmade textiles, antiques, jewelry, and, of course, the usual array of art books, posters, and note cards.

- **Research Departments:**
  The Art Reference Library, The
  Wilbour Library of Egyptology,
  The Brooklyn Museum Archives.
  Appointment necessary.

- **Public Programs:** Gallery talks,
  weekend drop-in programs for
  children, summer jazz concerts,
  film series, lectures. Call ahead
  for information.

Suggested 60-Minute Tour

*Begin on the fifth floor in the
American Painting and Sculpture
Galleries.*

Highlights

American Painting and Sculpture Galleries
Location: Fifth Floor

The American Painting and Sculpture Galleries house one of the finest collections of American art in the world. As you browse, look for important paintings by Raphael Peale, Winslow Homer, and Thomas Cole. In the contemporary (Seaver) galleries, look for works by later 20th-century masters like Richard Diebenkorn, David Smith, and others.

Edward Hicks
The Peaceable Kingdom,
c. 1833–34
Location: Fifth Floor, American
Painting and Sculpture Galleries

Jungle beasts, forest creatures, and farm animals mingle as happy friends in this charming painting by Edward Hicks. Alongside rest a small boy and girl, while in the distance is a portrayal of the return of William Penn surrounded by Indians. The artist has re-created, in visual form, a literal interpretation of the 11th chapter of Isaiah—"all men and beasts will live in peace." The artist made more than 100 paintings of this subject as an expression of his Quaker pacifist ideals.

As a young man Edward Hicks embraced the Quaker religion and became a preacher. His limited income forced him to take on additional work as a coach- and sign-painter, a dual role that ultimately caused him to feel a deep conflict beween the austerity of his Quaker beliefs and the pleasure he derived from painting. It has been suggested by historians that the anguished, staring eyes of the lion and leopard are an expression of his troubled conscience.

Hicks lived and worked in Bucks County, Pennsylvania, and is considered one of America's best-known primitive artists of the late 19th century.

What is "naive" or "primitive" art?

Edward Hicks (USA), Grandma Moses (USA), and Henri Rousseau (France) are among the well-known artists whose work is usually categorized as "naive" or "primitive." The terms are general, and apply to artists' styles that may share certain characteristics such as the use of bright colors, and figures that may appear literal or childlike or demonstrate a lack of the scientific sense of perspective. Often the term is associated with artists who have not had formal art training, although this is not necessarily true since many sophisticated artists have deliberately assumed a naive style.

Albert Bierstadt
*Storm in the Rocky Mountains,
Mount Rosalie,* c. 1866
Location: Fifth Floor, American
Painting and Sculpture Galleries

Threatening thunderclouds rush over
dramatic craggy mountaintops as
sunlight drenches the vast valley
below. In the foreground an Indian is
seen running after a frightened horse.
Barely visible near the stream's edge
is an abandoned campsite with bow
and arrows, and a deer carcass. The
figures are deliberately kept small to
contrast with the great size of the
mountains.

Bierstadt wrote that he was feeling glum on the day that he set out
to see Mount Rosalie, but that his
spirits lifted when he came upon this
spectacular scene. Although he had
planned to sketch for only a brief
period, he became so caught up in
the moment, he spent several hours
working on his preliminary drawings.

To create this grandiose view, he
worked from field sketches of the
Chicago Lakes area of the Colorado
Rockies which he visited in 1863. The
scene is not topographically accurate
but is actually a composite of several
mountain sites sketched by Bierstadt
during his excursion to the new
frontier.

Mount Rosalie (now Mount
Evans) was named in honor of the
wife of journalist Fitz Hugh Ludlow,
Bierstadt's traveling companion.
Bierstadt married her in 1886 follow-
ing her divorce from the writer.

Bierstadt's flamboyant personality
and theatrical marketing tactics made
him a very successful artist. For
example, before *Mount Rosalie* was
sold, the artist arranged for it to
travel to several major American cities
for special shows. Its arrival was
widely publicized ahead of time, and
when the painting finally went on
exhibition it was placed in a separate
gallery and festooned with colored
swags. There was a charge for admission, and patrons would remain for
long periods, examining every minute
detail with opera glasses. The painting was eventually sold to an English-
man, Sir Samuel Morton Peto, for
more than $25,000—a sum unheard
of for a work of art at that time.

Bierstadt, *Storm in the Rocky Mountains*

William Merritt Chase
In the Studio, c. 1881
Location: Fifth Floor, American
Painting and Sculpture Galleries

When William Merritt Chase took over the large New York City studio vacated by the well-known landscape artist, Albert Bierstadt, he turned it into a showplace where he could work and promote his art. *In the Studio* provides an intimate view of the interior.

A woman, perhaps a guest at one of Chase's famous Saturday open houses, is shown seated on a carved bench poring over a large volume of drawings. Color is everywhere—in the woven rug that graces the expanse of wooden floors, in the paintings hung in rows on the walls, and in the bric-a-brac that clutters an ornate sideboard. Chase creates a feeling of spaciousness by making the figure of the woman small, and the expanse of floor large. The suggestion of high ceilings is accomplished by cropping the walls at the top.

William Merritt Chase settled in New York City in 1878 after studying art in Munich. He taught at the Art Students League of New York and then established his own Chase School of Art in Manhattan. During his lifetime Chase produced at least 2,000 paintings in a wide range of subjects including portraits, landscapes, and interiors.

John Singer Sargent
*Paul Helleu Sketching
with His Wife,* 1889
Location: Fifth Floor, American
Painting and Sculpture Galleries

Sargent's delightful painting portrays a young couple relaxing in tall grass near a small red rowboat. The subjects are his friends, Paul Helleu, a French artist, and his bride. As Helleu dabs at his canvas, his young wife gazes dreamily into the distance. Their light-colored straw hats serve as a focal point to pull the viewer's eyes directly into the painting.

Chase, *In the Studio*

Sargent took a photo of this quiet scene when the young couple paid him a visit. He later used it as a model to work from in his studio, and gave them the completed painting as a gift.

From 1874 to 1878 Sargent took his artistic training in Paris, studying in the atelier Emile Caroulus-Duran. He enjoyed considerable success in Paris until his career was adversely affected by the scathing criticism given to his risqué painting of *Madame X* at the Paris Salon of 1884. Following this unfortunate downturn in his career, he moved to London. He spent his summers in the art colony of Broadway, a quiet area in the English countryside near Fladbury along the River Avon. It was here that *Paul Helleu Sketching with His Wife* was painted.

Georgia O'Keeffe
Brooklyn Bridge, 1948
Location: Fifth Floor, American Painting and Sculpture Galleries

By making a fragment of a much larger object the center of attention (in this case, the Brooklyn Bridge), O'Keeffe manages to change the way the image is understood by the viewer. This blown-up view makes the structure's arches appear as though they are pointed Gothic windows of a cathedral, while the cable webbing,

outlined against the blue sky, resembles stained glass.

Even though O'Keeffe is better known for her paintings of the flora and fauna of New Mexico, she had great affection for New York City, and in particular, for the Brooklyn Bridge, which she considered a modern icon.

Marsden Hartley
Painting #48, Berlin, 1913
Location: Fifth Floor, American Painting and Sculpture Galleries

In 1912, with the encouragement of the important New York art dealer-photographer Alfred Stieglitz, Marsden Hartley went to Paris to see contemporary works by European artists. There he met some of the most influential people in the art world—modernists such as Picasso, Cézanne, and Matisse—and participated in Leo and Gertrude Stein's famous salon parties, where he saw and discussed the latest trends in Parisian art. He was profoundly influenced by these experiences and became one of the first American artists to incorporate ideas about European modernism into his own work. During this period Hartley also established close friendships with young German artists. Inspired by them, and by his readings of Kandinsky's *On the Spiritual in Art*, he traveled to Germany and was impressed with the city's welcoming environment for young artists like himself.

It was during this six-month visit that he executed *Painting #48, Berlin.* The painting shows the effects of his exposure to European modernism: the collage of medals, gold-braid, and military patches are references to his fascination with Germany's pre-World War I military pageantry; Picasso's influence is demonstrated in the painting's many-faceted analytical Cubist style; and mystical symbolism appears in shapes, colors, and particularly numbers. Notice the number 8 that appears at the top, which Hartley associated with transcendence from the material to the spiritual.

Continue on to the Iris and B. Gerald Cantor Gallery (Location: Fifth Floor) to view sculptures by Rodin.
A stroll through this gallery is well worth a little extra time. The gallery is light-filled and spacious, with numerous examples of Rodin's finest works.

Auguste Rodin
Pierre de Weissant from *The Burghers of Calais*, c. 1886–87
Location: Fifth Floor, Cantor Gallery

The bronze representation of Pierre de Weissant is one of six figures that make up Rodin's famous group piece, The Burghers of Calais. The work in its entirety recalls a famous incident in Calais that occurred in the 14th century during the Hundred Years War, when 12 councilmen volunteered to surrender to the English King Edward III in order to save their beloved city from destruction. They were imprisoned, and while they awaited their fate, King Edward's pregnant wife begged the king to forego their punishment. Ultimately Edward spared them from death.

De Weissant is a powerful figure, as evidenced by his muscular torso and large hands. He is draped in loose sackcloth and a rope hangs over his shoulder as a reminder of his fate as a prisoner.

It took Rodin four years to complete the entire group. He wanted the work installed at ground level in the plaza at Calais to dramatize its impact on the viewer. However, the Calais city fathers had other ideas and decided to place the composition on a high pedestal to soften the emotional intensity of the work.

Continue on to the Beatrice and Samuel A. Seaver Gallery of Contemporary Art, also on the fifth floor.

Richard Diebenkorn
Ocean Park, Number 27, 1970
Location: Fifth Floor, Seaver Gallery

Diebenkorn's abstraction of the California coastline was created by using a technique of taping, painting, and scraping hued pigments. What emerges is a compressed montage of colored geometric shapes that relate to the landscape around Santa Monica where the artist's studio was located: the greens and blues of sky and sea, the lavenders and golds of the California terrain, the lines that simulate roadways crisscrossing the countryside, and most of all, the sense of pure light that saturates everything.

David Smith
The Hero, 1952
Location: Fifth Floor, Seaver Gallery

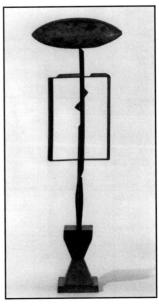

David Smith's geometric abstraction of a female figure is balanced on a two-part pedestal. It has a rectangle for its torso, two small triangles that represent breasts, and a tank top for its head, which resembles an elongated football. *The Hero* was the prototype for ten or more sculptural works by Smith known as the *Tanktotem Series.* The word "Tank" refers to the industrial tank lids that he used for heads and "totem" may be a reference to a literary work by Sigmund Freud, *Totem and Tattoo,* which greatly influenced the artist. Freud's premise was that a male's clan name is attached to, and becomes synonymous with, the forbidden female. It has been suggested that this is the reason the artist applied the word "hero" to a female figure.

Smith began studying art at Ohio University in 1924. In the summer of 1925 he worked at the Studebaker factory in South Bend, Indiana, where he acquired skills in metalwork that he later put to use in his career as a sculptor. He also studied painting at the Art Student's League in New York. He is known for his constructions from steel and "found" scrap parts, which often resembled calligraphic forms. His later monumental works consisted of boxes and cylinders of polished metal. Smith is recognized as one of the most imaginative and influential American sculptors of the 20th century.

Continue on to the Decorative Arts Department, located on the fourth floor.

The Brooklyn Museum has one of the most complete collections of American decorative arts in the world, with 28 American period rooms including a 1675 Dutch-American home, colonial dining rooms, 19th-century parlors, sitting rooms, and even an Art Deco Library circa 1920. Also on display are ceramics, glass, silver, and furniture.

Hall, The Cupola House, c. 1725
Location: Fourth Floor, American Period Rooms

This handsome "hall" is from a house built by Richard Sanderson around 1725 in Edenton, North Carolina. It was later remodeled by a subsequent owner, Francis Corbin, between 1756–58.

Painted a stunning Prussian blue, the room is arranged as though its owner is about to give an elegant dinner party. Exquisite Chippendale furniture, English pottery, imported glass, silver, and Chinese porcelain are placed around the room. Of particular interest is the outstanding example of a floorcovering painted to resemble marble inlaid tiles in shades of green, gold, and brown. The durable canvas throws were commonly placed in heavily used areas instead of woven rugs.

John D. Rockefeller House, Moorish Smoking Room, c. 1883
Location: Fourth Floor, American Period Rooms

This room is distinctive, not only because of the elaborate completeness of the Moorish design, but also because it is a superb example of a room reflecting a specific environment or feeling of another time and place.

In the latter part of the 19th century, contact with the Middle East increased and people became quite fascinated with exotic cultures and the uniqueness of their designs in textiles, furnishings, and architecture. Eventually these designs were popularized and began to appear in the homes of the well-to-do, especially in European countries. Taken as a whole, every aspect of the Moorish Smoking Room represents these trends. Oriental rugs, sinuous, swirling patterns on the wallpaper, rich colors on upholstered furniture and draperies are all variations of Moorish and Middle Eastern motifs. There's even a hookah to add a touch of authenticity.

The Jan Martense Schenck House, c. 1675
Location: Fourth Floor, American Period Rooms

This Early American house, built by a well-to-do Dutch miller in the latter part of the 17th century, originally stood in the Brooklyn flatlands. The structure once had an upstairs sleeping loft and grain storage area. Represented here are the two ground floor rooms as they may have appeared after they underwent remodeling in 1730.

The main room or "hall" was used for everyday living, eating, and social-izing. Note the large open hearth with a chimney cloth around it, a typ-ical Dutch feature. Heavy exposed beams and bare floors that were cleaned by scrubbing with sand were also typical, reflecting medieval European structural traditions. The north room is installed as the parlor and contains precious mementos including the *kas,* or wardrobe, one of the family's most valued pieces of furniture imported from the Netherlands.

The Brooklyn Museum showcases another house built around 1775 by Nicholas Schenck, the grandson of Jan Martense Schenck.

Continue on to the Ancient Egyptian and Middle Eastern Galleries (Location: Third Floor).

In spacious galleries you'll find great treasures from ancient Egyptian tombs, and royal cities of the Pre-Dynastic period, including exquisitely decorated mummy cases, statues of kings and queens, sacred animals, and more. In the Ancient Middle Eastern Galleries browsers can enjoy massive storytelling wall carvings, ancient pottery, and other precious objects.

Mummy Cartonnage of Nespanetjerenpere (c. 945–715 B.C.) and of Sesostris III (c. 1878–1840 B.C.)
Location: Third Floor, Ancient Egyptian Art Galleries

In ancient times Egyptians created elaborately decorated containers, called cartonnage, into which a mum-mified body was placed. This was then stored within another coffin or sarcophagus. The materials used to make the cartonnage were linen or papyrus mixed with plaster. Facial characteristics were then applied, such as eyes, lips, and eyebrows, often dramatically enhanced with lapis lazuli and bits of glass.

Egyptians would incorporate into their depiction of the deceased many symbols that related to his or her life and accomplishments. For example, shown on Nespanetjerenpere's face is a braided sacred beard that suggests an association with the gods. On the back of the mummy case, raising the *ankh* (the emblem of life), are the deities—Thoth, the scribe, and Horus, the falcon-headed man. Also shown is the god Osiris, king and judge of the dead, who is bearded and wears the *atef* crown.

Ibis Coffin, Ptolemaic period, gilded wood, crystal, silver, gold, c. 330–305 B.C.
Location: Third Floor, Ancient Egyptian Art Galleries

Animals and birds sacred to various deities were often mummified and buried in special cemeteries. This stunning silver- and golden-hued coffin, believed to have come from the Egyptian animal cemetery at Tuna el-Gebel, was made to hold the remains of the sacred ibis. It assumes the bird's shape with beak, head, neck, and legs of silver, eyes of rock crystal, and body in overlaid gilt.

The ibis, the most sacred Egyptian bird, symbolized the god Thoth. Like the Greek god Hermes,

Thoth was associated with wisdom and learning and was considered the creator of all languages. He is often depicted with a tally sheet recording in *The Book of the Dead* as he measures and compares the weight of the dead person's heart against the feather of truth.

Winged Genie from Palace at Nimrud, Assyria (Reign of Ashurnasirpal II, c. 883–859 B.C.)
Location: Third Floor, Ancient Middle Eastern Art Galleries

This stone relief portrays the bird-faced Winged Genie as a powerful figure with bulging muscles in his calves and forearms. Attached to his weighty body is a set of finely carved wings, and his beard and long hair are precisely braided into neat rows. He wears an elegant fringed shawl over a tunic and displays a rosette headband, bracelets that resemble stylized watches, and other jewelry including earrings and a beaded necklace. The pail held in his left hand may have been used to hold liquid to bless a "Sacred Tree," a venerated symbol of the Assyrians. These winged humanoid creatures are believed to represent ritual helpers of the king.

In keeping with the traditions of Assyrian art, the relief also has cuneiform inscriptions that tell of the heroic exploits of Assyrian rulers.

African Art Galleries

Newly refurbished galleries on the first floor show off one of America's most important collections of African art. The Brooklyn Museum was the first to exhibit African art as art rather than artifacts of ethnological interest alone. This has been an

ongoing tradition since its first exhibit in 1923. Rotating exhibition space is now provided to focus on specific topics and highlight recent acquisitions.

Hornblower, 17th century, Nigeria
Location: First Floor, African Art Galleries

This figure of a male courtier blowing a small horn is a distinguished example of the famous bronzes of the Benin Kingdom of southern Nigeria. Only the king could request the making of objects from casters. The king (*oba*) would have kept this object in a place of honor on the altar of a forefather. Notice the finely engraved designs on the clothing: the circle surrounded by leaves is a design associated with the river leaves of Olokun, god of the waters. The leopards' heads shown on the skirt front symbolize the power of the *oba*.

Kuba Mask (*moshambwooy*), 19th century, Zaire
Location: First Floor, African Art Galleries

Recently restored and newly on display is this compelling and complex Kuba ceremonial mask. Beads and shells give definition to the facial features, long hair provides the beard, and animal hide, metal, paint, cotton, and other fibers decorate and bind the whole together.

Bom Bosh (*ndop*), mid-18th century, Zaire
Location: First Floor, African Art Galleries

Bom Bosh was the first king of the Kuba people to be recognized as both spiritual and political leader. The figure functions as a commemorative work, created 100 years after his reign. It is the oldest of eleven similar figures known to exist, making it an especially treasured work of art.

This is not an actual likeness of Bom Bosh. Rather, the corpulent Kuba king is an effigy, and as such, shares common attributes with other representations of royalty: a belt and armband showing cowrie shell designs; a drum with a severed hand that refers to the king's fame as a military leader; a visor-like hairstyle; an official knife held in his hand; and a decorated platform.

Illustrations

p. 18: Brooklyn Museum, exterior

p. 24: Edward Hicks, *The Peaceable Kingdom*, circa 1840–45. Oil on canvas. 18″ × 24⅛″ (45.8 × 61.2 cm). The Brooklyn Museum, Acc. #40.340. Dick S. Ramsay Fund.

p. 25: Albert Bierstadt, *Storm in the Rocky Mountains, Mt. Rosalie*, 1866. Oil on canvas. 83″ × 142¼″ (210.8 × 361.3 cm). The Brooklyn Museum, Acc. #76.79. Dick S. Ramsay Fund; A. Augustus Healy Fund;

Frank L. Babbot Fund. Photograph courtesy of the Brooklyn Museum.

p. 26: William Merritt Chase, *In the Studio*, circa 1880. Oil on canvas. 20¹/₈″ × 40¹/₁₆″ (71.4 × 101.8 cm). The Brooklyn Museum, Acc. #13.50. Gift of Mrs. Carll H. DeSilver in memory of her husband. Photograph courtesy of the Brooklyn Museum.

p. 27: (top left) John Singer Sargent, *Paul Helleu Sketching with His Wife*, 1889. Oil on canvas. 26¹/₈″ × 32¹/₈″. The Brooklyn Museum, Acc. #20.640. Museum Collection Fund. Photograph courtesy of the Brooklyn Museum.

p. 27: (top right) Georgia O'Keeffe, *Brooklyn Bridge*, 1948. Oil on masonite. 47¹⁵/₁₆″ × 35⁷/₈″ (121.8 × 91.0 cm). The Brooklyn Museum, Acc. #77.11. Bequest of Mary Childs Draper. Photograph courtesy of the Brooklyn Museum.

p. 27: (bottom right) Marsden Hartley, *Painting #48, Berlin*, 1913. Oil on canvas. 47³/₁₆″ × 47³/₁₆″. The Brooklyn Museum, Acc. #58.158. Dick S. Ramsay Fund. Photograph courtesy of the Brooklyn Museum.

p. 28: Auguste Rodin, *Pierre de Weissant*, circa 1886–87. Bronze, cast 1979. 84⁵/₈″ × 46″ × 39″. The Brooklyn Museum, Acc. #84.210.9. Gift of Iris and B. Gerald Cantor. Photograph courtesy of the Brooklyn Museum.

p. 29: David Smith, *The Hero*, 1952. Steel. 73¹¹/₁₆″ × 25¹/₂″ × 11³/₄″. The Brooklyn Museum, Acc. #57.185. Dick S. Ramsay

Fund. Photo by Faith Gooden, courtesy of the Brooklyn Museum.

p. 30: *The Moorish Smoking Room, The John D. Rockefeller House*, New York City, N.Y. Built in 1864–65. The Brooklyn Museum, Acc. #46.43. Gift of Mr. John D. Rockefeller, Jr. and John D. Rockefeller, III. Photograph courtesy of the Brooklyn Museum.

p. 31: *Mummy Cartonnage of Nespanetjerenpere*, Egypt, Thebes, Third Intermediate Period, probably Dynasty XXII (945–718 B.C. Cartonnage of linen or papyrus mixed with plaster, inlaid with glass and lapis lazuli. 69³/₄″ high (177 cm). The Brooklyn Museum, Acc. #35.1265. Charles Edwin Wilbour Fund. Photograph courtesy of the Brooklyn Museum.

p. 32: *Standing Figure of an Ibis* (serving as Container for mummified Ibis), Ptolemaic period, 330–305 B.C. Wood, gilt, paint, rock crystal, silver. Length from tip of tail to beak: 23¹/₂″ × 15″ (58.7 × 38.2 cm). The Brooklyn Museum, Acc. #49.48. Charles Edwin Wilbour Fund. Photograph courtesy of the Brooklyn Museum.

p. 33: *Kuba Mask*, late 19th–early 20th century. Bark cloth, pigment, shell, beads, hair, fabric. 19⁵/₁₆″ × 14⁹/₁₆″. The Brooklyn Museum, Acc. #22.1582. Museum Expedition 1922, Robert B. Woodward Memorial Fund. Photograph courtesy of the Brooklyn Museum.

Ellis Island Immigration Museum

Address:
New York Harbor
New York, New York 10004
(212) 363-7620
(212) 363-3200 recorded information
(212) 269-5755 ferry information

Hours:
Open: Daily 9–5. Extended hours
during the summer.
Note: Third floor closes at
4:30. Begin your tour there
if you arrive in the late
afternoon.
Closed: Christmas

Entry Fees:
Free. Donations appreciated.

Type:
History of immigration
into the United States

Transportation:
Subway: 1, 4, 5, 9, N, R
to Battery Park,
then take Circle Line Ferry.
Bus: M1, M6, M15
to Battery Park,
then take Circle Line Ferry.

Museum Shop:
Yes. Gift items, posters, mementos
reflecting immigrants' homelands.

Restaurant:
Yes. Ellis Island Cafe.

Disabled Access:
Yes

1st Floor

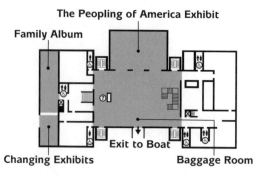

The Peopling of America Exhibit

Family Album

Changing Exhibits

Exit to Boat

Baggage Room

2nd Floor

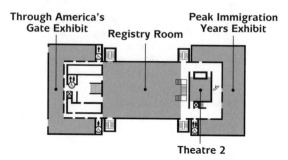

Through America's Gate Exhibit

Registry Room

Peak Immigration Years Exhibit

Theatre 2

3rd Floor

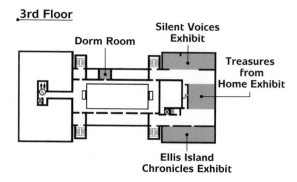

Dorm Room

Silent Voices Exhibit

Treasures from Home Exhibit

Ellis Island Chronicles Exhibit

This floor plan highlights only the areas included in the suggested tour.
A detailed floor plan of the museum is available at the Information Desk.

What to Expect

Since its restoration and reopening on September 10, 1990, the Ellis Island Immigration Museum has become one of the most popular places to visit in New York City. The Museum occupies the building which once served as the major immigration processing center for the United States on a small island located just a few hundred yards north of the Statue of Liberty. This structure, opened in 1892, served as the first point of entry for more than half of all the immigrants who sought entry to the United States. The center, which finally closed in 1954, received and processed over 16 million settlers from foreign countries, and today it's estimated that 40% of Americans can trace their ancestry to immigrants who entered through Ellis Island.

Inside the enormous main building you'll find displays on three floors devoted to the saga of immigration into the United States. As the story unfolds, you are able to see, feel, and appreciate every aspect of the immigration experience from the time individuals and families left their homeland to their arrival at Ellis Island. You'll visit the large registry room where immigrants were processed, and see an array of exhibits that show how the facility expanded over the years to handle this human deluge. Photo displays, memorabilia, and taped firsthand accounts from immigrants dramatize their experiences, while an interactive information center and changing exhibitions focus on a variety of immigration themes.

Facts

■ *The turn of the 20th century marks the period when the greatest number of immigrants arrived at Ellis Island. It was not unusual for staffers to process as many as 5,000 people a day. The peak was reached in 1907 when over 11,700 people were processed in one day!*

■ *Men made up the majority of immigrants entering America. They would come seeking economic opportunities, jobs, and homes. As they became established they would send for their families.*

■ *The greatest number of immigrants passing through Ellis Island were Italians, with over 2.5 million entries between 1892–1931. Russians came in second with 1.8 million entries in roughly the same time period. Austrians, Germans, English, and Irish also came in huge numbers. Today over 100 million Americans can trace their ancestry to immigrants who were processed at Ellis Island.*

Begin your visit by viewing the inspirational video, *Island of Hope/Island of Tears*. If you're in a hurry, the following suggestions are acknowledged popular favorites.

FIRST FLOOR

* ***Island of Hope/Island of Tears:***
A short film by the Oscar-winning filmmaker, Charles Guggenheim, in which immigrants tell inspiring stories about leaving their homelands and coming to America. Shown in two theaters on the first and second floors.

* **Baggage Exhibit:** Countless battered trunks, carpetbags, and parcels of all sizes and variety recall this area's original purpose. Before immigrants climbed the stairs to The Great Hall, they were urged to check their baggage. But many refused, not wanting to part with their last material contact with the homeland. They had to keep track of it during the lengthy examinations that followed.

Peopling of America

* **Peopling of America:** Located in the old railroad ticket office, graphic displays trace the history of immigration from pre-Colonial times to the present. Be sure to see the *Faces of America* exhibit with thousands of faces of Americans seen from one direction, and the American flag seen from the other. Also, you can use a computer to view names of those who donated to the American Immigrant Wall of Honor.

The Learning Center: Here you will find state-of-the art technology that helps teach youngsters about their ancestry.

SECOND FLOOR

* **Registry Room (also called The Great Hall):** It was here that immigrants' entry into America was allowed or denied. Although it appears large and empty today (200 feet long by 100 feet wide), often the room was extremely crowded, hot, and smelly. Would-be citizens went through a process in which they were interviewed and underwent physical examinations. Their entry hung in the balance, and those proclaimed ill or disabled were sent back to Europe alone.

* **Through America's Gate:** Fourteen rooms of exhibits where you can see and experience the immigration process. Fascinating displays of photographs, documents, and recorded memories told by immigrants bring to life the joy, the uncertainties, and the aspirations associated with the immigrants' journey to a new land. One fascinating exhibit demonstrates how officials conducted intelligence tests. People who were thought to have limited or nonexistent educational backgrounds were asked to draw a diamond, with widely varied results; other tests included matching patterns and assembling blocks on which faces with varying expressions were depicted.

Registry Room

* **Peak Immigration Years:** Browse through several rooms of exhibits that demonstrate through photographs, passports, posters, and other memorabilia, the trials, tribulations, and triumphs of immigrants, no matter what their port of entry, and their assimilation into mainstream America.

THIRD FLOOR

* **Treasures from Home:** On display is a poignant collection of over 1,000 personal belongings donated or loaned to the Museum by the families of immigrants. Everything from clothing to cooking utensils, prayer books and bibles, a long-stemmed pipe and a samovar were brought over by settlers from abroad not knowing what to expect.

Silent Voices: Photographs and mementos that depict Ellis Island in its abandoned state.

Restoring a Landmark: Transformation of Ellis Island from its abandoned state to a museum.

* **Dormitory Room:** This long, narrow room, used as accommodations for detained immigrants, offers a sense of the confinement endured by those waiting to be admitted. In the early 1900s the men's and women's dormitories could accommodate up to three hundred people, with families and single immigrants sharing the same space. It wasn't until 1924 that the original canvas bunks were replaced by single beds, and families were assigned to private rooms.

OUTSIDE

American Immigrant Wall of Honor: The world's largest wall of names, with 420,000 immigrants listed including Miles Standish, Priscilla Alden, George Washington's grandfather, and President John F. Kennedy's great-grandparents. The view back toward Manhattan Island is one of the best, and this is a great place to take photographs.

Treasures from Home

Looking back: *If your ancestors entered through Ellis Island, their journey to the United States would have been by boat. Upon arrival, the process of gaining entry began immediately. First- and second-class travelers, who had paid higher passenger fees, were processed aboard ship before they landed, under fairly decent conditions. For those in steerage class, however, entry into this country was far more arduous. They were required to undergo physical examinations on shipboard under very cramped conditions. Once on the island, they were crammed into The Great Hall to await an appearance before federal immigration authorities. Here they were closely observed, underwent questioning, and were given yet another physical examination by health officials to screen out those with contagious diseases, especiallly cholera, typhoid fever, and smallpox. Those who were thought to have these or other physical or mental problems were placed in quarantine. Finally, after many hours, even days of processing, usually in hot and crowded conditions, the newcomers received permission to enter the country. Women immigrants traveling alone were not permitted entry until a male relative came to claim them. Those unlucky enough to have their entry denied were separated from loved ones and sent back to their homeland.*

Illustrations

The Metropolitan Museum of Art

Horace Pippin

I tell my heart

Address:
Fifth Avenue at East 82nd Street
(Manhattan, Upper East Side)
New York, New York 10028
(212) 879-5500
(212) 535-7710 recorded information

Hours:
Open: Friday–Saturday 9:30–8:45;
        Sunday, Tuesday, Wednesday,
        Thursday 9:30–5:15
Closed: Monday, Thanksgiving,
        Christmas, New Year's Day

Entry Fees:
Yes, includes Main Building and
The Cloisters on the same day;
free for members and children
under 12 with an adult.

Type:
Art

Transportation:
Subway: 4, 5, 6
Bus: M1, M2, M3, M4, M18, M79

Museum Shop:
Yes, two located off the Great Hall,
one on second floor off the Great
Hall balcony

Restaurant:
Yes. Museum Cafeteria, Museum
Dining Room; hours vary here; for
reservations call (212) 570-3964

Disabled Access:
Yes. Entrance at 5th Avenue and 81st
Street and at museum parking garage;
wheelchairs at coat-check area.

Extras:
For programs and other information
for sight and hearing impaired visitors,
call Disabled Visitors Services (212)
535-7710 or TTY (212) 879-0421.

1st Floor

American Wing
"Garden Court," Period Rooms, Paintings

Arms and Armor

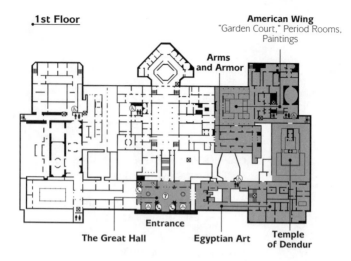

Entrance

The Great Hall

Egyptian Art

Temple of Dendur

2nd Floor

American Wing
Paintings

European Painting

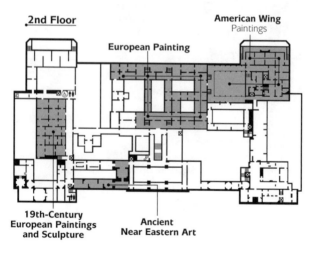

19th-Century European Paintings and Sculpture

Ancient Near Eastern Art

This floor plan highlights only the areas included in the suggested tours.
A detailed floor plan of the museum is available at the Information Desk.

What to Expect

The Metropolitan Museum of Art (or The Met, as the locals refer to it) is New York City's most popular tourist attraction, with more than 4 million people flocking through its galleries annually. Considered one of the world's finest art museums, its collections include more than two million works of art spanning 5,000 years of world culture from prehistory to the present.

The Metropolitan's more than 3,000 European paintings form one of the greatest such collections in the world. Old Masters such as Rembrandt, Vermeer, and Goya are among the best, not to mention the Impressionist and Post-Impressionist masterpieces. There are 4,000 separate objects in the medieval collections, and virtually all of the 50,000 objects in the world-class Egyptian collection are on display. The American collection, situated in its own wing, showcases the world's most comprehensive collection of American paintings and sculpture, and 24 period rooms, filled with furnishings and decorative objects, offer intimate views of American domestic life from early colonial times to Frank Lloyd Wright. Other major collections include arms and armor, European sculpture and decorative arts, costumes, Asian art, musical instruments, and 20th-century art.

The Met is not only large, it's also friendly. There are many places to sit and relax in its galleries and beautiful interior spaces like the Petrie Sculpture Court or the American Wing Garden Court. Two restaurants serve a variety of food and beverages, and on Fridays and Saturdays between 4 and 8:30 P.M. you can sit in the balcony overlooking the Great Hall, have a glass of wine, and listen to live music.

The scale of the building is so large and the collections are so vast that you shouldn't attempt to see everything in one visit. Do, however, try to browse awhile, for one of the great pleasures of visiting the Met is coming upon unexpected surprises.

Special Information

- **Guided tours** in English daily. Inquire at Information Desk for times. Free with admission are individual tours in French, Italian, Japanese, and Spanish.

- **Group tours** by appointment in English, French, Italian, Japanese, Spanish, and other languages. Advance reservations required. Call (212) 570-3711.

- **Acoustiguides:** Recorded tours of the Met's collections and special exhibitions. Ask at desk for information.

- **International Visitors Desk:** Located in the Great Hall. Maps, brochures, tour information in Chinese, French, German, Italian, Japanese, and Spanish.

- **A major renovation program** is in progress and some galleries are subject to closure or will have a temporary change in location. Check at the main desk for current information.

- **Gallery schedule:** Due to cutbacks in funding, some galleries are open to the public on an alternating schedule. Check at the Information Desk for specifics.

- **The Costume Department,** located downstairs, has several special exhibitions every year. Check at the Information Desk for details.

- **For children,** strollers permitted every day except Sunday. Back carriers available at 81st Street entrance. Fun museum trail maps for kids are provided at the Information Desk.

- **The Iris and B. Gerald Cantor Roof Garden,** situated above the Wallace Wing, not only contains one of the most exciting collections of 20th-century sculpture, but has one of the most spectacular views of Manhattan. The Roof Garden can be reached by elevator. Check at the Information Desk first.

- **Programs:** Lectures, films, concerts, and other programs. Schedules available at the Information Desk.

- **The Cloisters,** the Metropolitan Museum's branch for Medieval Art, is located in Fort Tryon Park at the northern tip of Manhattan.

Suggested 60-Minute Tour

Two tours are suggested.

Tour 1: *Samplings from the first and second floors include the Arms and Armor Collection, the American Wing Decorative Arts Collection, the American Wing Paintings and Sculpture Collection (first and second floors), and the Egyptian Collection.*

Tour 2: *Samplings from the second floor include the European Paintings Collection, the Nineteenth-Century European Paintings Collection (Impressionists), and Ancient Near Eastern Art.*

Remember to get a complimentary museum floor plan at the Visitors Desk in the Great Hall.

TOUR 1: Begin in the Arms and Armor Galleries. To reach this area, walk past the bookstore, enter the Medieval Art area, then turn right, walk through the European Sculpture and Decorative Arts Galleries, and finally into the Arms and Armor Galleries.

The Arms and Armor Collection is one of the most popular in the Metropolitan Museum, with both adults and children enjoying ten spacious galleries filled with thousands of swords, shields, pistols, suits of armor, and various other war paraphernalia. The collection has 14,000 objects from Europe, the Near East, the Far East, and the Americas. Look for the following special attractions.

Parade Sallet (Helmet), Italy, c. 1460

A battle helmet, cleverly disguised as a lion's head, is fashioned from gilt bronze with eyes that sparkle with inset carnelian stones. The helmet is said to resemble the one worn by Hercules and refers to the slaying of the lion of Nemea by strangulation. Anyone wearing this helmet would have been identified with the victories of the strong and the triumph of right over wrong.

German Parade Rapier, Dresden, c. 1606

Made for Christian II, Duke of Saxony, and elector of the Holy Roman Empire, this exquisite sword handle (hilt) is lavishly covered with allegorical figures and sparkling jewels and pearls. Although made originally as a decorative object not intended for battle, it may actually have been used by the Duke to defend his life in a skirmish during the Thirty Years War (1618–48).

Armor of George Clifford, Third Earl of Cumberland, England, c. 1580–85

Among the most spectacular objects in the Met is this suit of armor worn by the third Earl of Cumberland when he participated in grand tournaments held before Queen Elizabeth I. Made from steel plates held together with rivets and pins for flexibility at the joints, the armor is put on in sections and held together with leather straps.

The Earl's armor was designed and crafted in Greenwich, England, at the royal armor workshops. The elaborate decorations, etched into the metal in gold, include the Tudor rose, the double E (for Elizabeth), and the *fleur-de-lis*.

Armed Horses and Knights, c. 1500

This dazzling group of prancing horses and knights, clad in European armor, is one of the Metropolitan Museum's most popular displays. The lead horseman is dressed in German jousting armor and has his lance raised as if to charge the enemy. The horse is carefully padded to avoid injury and also blindfolded to prevent it from shying.

The warhorses were bred for size and strength, stamina and courage, and were highly trained. Among the better known of these breeds are the Percheron, Belgian, Shire, and Clydesdale. They were trained to trot when the knight gave signals with his legs. The warhorse did not gallop, however, because it was difficult for the knight to maneuver the horse while wearing so much armor.

Continue on to the American Wing, which is directly adjacent to the Arms and Armor Galleries.

The American Wing Decorative Arts Galleries consist of 24 spectac-ular rooms situated near the Ameri-can Wing Garden Court. Rooms are arranged with furnishings and objects to give a sense of how homes might

American Wing Garden Court

have looked in the past. As you browse, look for period furniture by Duncan Phyfe, a silver tea set by the venerable Paul Revere, and an early telegraph machine. Be sure to see the two rooms listed below.

Gallery 127
Frank Lloyd Wright
Living Room from the Little House, Wayzata, Minnesota, 1912–15

The room has many features associated with Wright's Prairie Style houses in which he first incorporated his concept of total design for interiors. Note, for example, how the reddish-brown bricks of the fireplace, the copper finish of the windows, the natural oak floors, and room trim blend together. Wright also designed many of the furnishings, placing them in small groupings around the room, allowing a large open space to remain

at its center. Long, horizontal lines characterize the architectural style, while Japanese prints and flower arrangements represent Wright's decorative preferences.

Gallery 303 (Upstairs)
Parlor from the Thomas Hart House (built before 1674)

The Hart Parlor is taken from an authentic 17th-century American dwelling. The low-ceilinged room, complete with its original beams, fireplace, and furnishings, was transferred to the Met from its original site in Ipswich, Massachusetts. The furnishings, of Flemish influence popular in England in the 1600s, include an ornately carved sideboard, a Brewster-type chair with lathe-turned spindles of hickory and ash, a side chair called a "William and Mary," and a table-chair, a cleverly designed piece of furniture made to serve two

Frank Lloyd Wright Living Room

purposes. The room was used as a place to sleep, to cook, and to socialize.

Continue on to the American Wing Paintings Galleries, directly adjacent to the American Wing Garden Court. The galleries occupy both the first and second floors. Expect to ramble a bit to find the following selections.

John Singer Sargent
Madame X (Madame Pierre Gautreau), 1883–1884 (Mezzanine)

Elegantly posed and wearing a clingy black low-cut gown, this striking portrait was considered quite sensational in its time. The subject, Judith

Avegno, was born in New Orleans and married a French banker. She was considered one of Paris's great beauties in the 1880s.

When Sargent met Madame Gautreau in 1881, he was so fascinated by her beauty, her vivaciousness, and her penchant for wearing lavender theatrical makeup that he wanted to paint her portrait immediately. It took him several years to complete the painting, however. When it was finally presented at the Paris Salon in 1884, under the title *Portrait de Mme...*, the reviews were scathing. Critics, attacking the portrait for being too risqué, made derogatory comments about her dress with its deep décolletage, and the lavender hue of her skin. Madame Gautreau's mother demanded the portrait be removed from the competition, but Sargent refused, furthering the intensity of the uproar. This proved to be costly for the artist; the negative publicity led to a decline in commissions and he eventually abandoned the Paris art scene and moved to London.

William M. Harnett
Still Life—Violin and Music (Music and Good Luck), 1888 (Balcony 224)

Still Life, at first glance, appears as a simple and straightforward arrangement, with a violin, a flute, a sheet of music, and a good-luck horseshoe arranged in a vertical format. On closer inspection, however, you'll notice numerous realistic textures and tones attributed to each object: the wood of the old violin glows, its strings glimmer, with painstakingly painted drops of rosin dust on the surface below; the sheet music and calling card have bent edges that seem real enough to touch; and the convincing shadows cast by the partially open door suggest depth. Heavy items suspended on strings or balanced precariously on nails take on a three-dimensional appearance.

Harnett specialized in *trompe l'oeil* (a French term meaning "deceives the eye"). This technique, which fools the viewer into believing that objects are real, requires great technical skill. His popular subject matter and technical brilliance made him one of the most widely copied still-life painters of his generation. It was not until after his death, however, that he received great critical acclaim and recognition.

Gilbert Stuart
George Washington (The Gibbs-Channing-Avery Portrait), 1795 (Gallery 113)

Washington was 63 years old when this familiar-looking portrait was painted. He is shown against a pleasant green background, wearing a brown coat and appearing distinguished and authoritative. There are at least 18 known copies of this pose, known as the "Vaughan type." It takes its name from the painting's original owner, Samuel Vaughan, an English merchant living in Philadelphia, and a close friend of Washington's.

Two other portraits of Washington that were produced by Gilbert Stuart hang in the American Paintings Galleries: another "Vaughan type" (the Phillips-Brixy bequest, c. 1798) showing Washington in a black coat set against a Venetian red background, and the Athaneum portrait (the Carroll-Havemeyer portrait, c. 1803), which is one of about 72 copies known to exist. Stuart often referred to his portraits of Washington as his "hundred dollar bills," a not-so-subtle way of stating their price.

Emanuel Leutze
Washington Crossing the Delaware, 1851 (Gallery 223)

Washington is portrayed with several of his soldiers standing on a flat-bottomed boat on its way into battle

Leutze, *Washington Crossing the Delaware*

across an ice-clogged river. The scene represents an historic event that took place on Christmas Eve, 1776, when Washington and 2,500 men made an attack on the Hessians at Trenton, a battle considered a turning point in the American Revolution.

Historians have shown that several of the details are erroneously represented, making the painting inaccurate as a document. For example, the action is shown in daylight, but records prove that the battle took place at night. Also, the boat that the soldiers stand in is incorrect; the real boats were heavy flat-bottomed "Durhams," made from iron. The craft shown in the painting would have been too light to hold Washington's troops. Furthermore, the soldiers' uniforms are incorrectly depicted, and the American flag is a version that was not adopted until six months after the Battle of Trenton. Despite these inaccuracies, the painting captured the spirit of the moment and the imagination of the nation, making it one of the best-known and best-loved images in American art. *Washington Crossing the Delaware* is the largest painting at the Metropolitan, measuring 12′5″ by 21′3″.

Leutze's first version of this painting was started in 1849 but suffered fire damage in his Dusseldorf studio. The following year, Leutze finished a second version (the one now owned by the Metropolitan). This was put on exhibition in New York in 1851 and sold to Marshall O. Roberts for the then-enormous sum of $10,000.

Albert Bierstadt
The Rocky Mountains, Landers Peak, 1863 (Gallery 221)

Bierstadt's large painting is a dazzling concoction of nature, complete with majestic mountain ranges, waterfalls, a glimmering lake, and an Indian camp. As though to prove his presence before such grandeur, the artist included his abandoned camera on a tripod in the foreground.

This painting resulted from Bierstadt's first trip to the West in 1859 when he accompanied a government survey expedition to the Nebraska Territory led by Frederick W. Lander. The location is what is actually Fremont Peak, part of the Wind River Range of the Rocky Mountains, in territory that later became the state of Wyoming.

Upon his return home, Bierstadt used his sketches and photos of the mountain range as models to create this painting in his studio. It received great acclaim when put on public exhibition, and was subsequently purchased by James McHenry, an American living in London, for the then-exhorbitant sum of $25,000. The artist later bought it back and gave or sold it to his brother, Edward.

Continue on to our final stop, the Egyptian Collection, which is located downstairs directly off of the Great Hall.

The Egyptian Collection is one of the best collections outside of Egypt. The galleries are arranged chronologically beginning with the Pre-Dynastic period (about 3100 B.C., before writing was developed) and ending with the Coptic period (8th century A.D.). The Egyptian mummy galleries are especially popular.

Outer Coffin of Henettaway,
c. 1000 B.C., Dynasty 21
Location: Mummy Galleries 21–25

Henettaway's coffin was found in a family tomb at Thebes at Deir al Bahri. Her remains were preserved and tightly wrapped and placed inside this elaborately decorated mummy case fashioned from gessoed and painted wood. She is shown wearing a three-part wig with two sidelocks and elaborate jewelry. Over the remainder of the mummy case are precisely painted designs—all with symbolic meanings. A large sky-goddess with outspread wings dominates the chest; alongside are mysterious eyes, also called the *Ka*, symbols of protection for the soul of the deceased. Note also the images of Anubis, the jackal-headed god of embalming who watched over the dead.

Coffin of Nephthys, 1850 B.C.
Location: Mummy Galleries 21–25

This mummy case incorporates painted decorations, inlaid stones, and gold leaf. It is of particular interest because of its distinctive red face. No, it's not blushing! The discoloration occurred because silver was added to the gold leaf, causing it to tarnish.

Queen Hatshepsut Enthroned,
c. 1485 B.C.
Location: Gallery 12

The life-size seated Queen, a lovely limestone statue known as the White Hatshepsut, appears elegant, quiet, and regal. She wears the traditional Egyptian royal wig with the characteristic wing-like protrusions on the sides of her head. Hatshepsut succeeded her half-brother husband,

Thutmose II, to the throne of Egypt following his death. You can see damage on the statue, thought to have been deliberately executed on the orders of her ambitious stepson, Thutmose III.

Hatshepsut came to the Metropolitan's collection in several parts. Her head and arm fragments were discovered during excavations in Deir al Bahri in 1928. Her body, which was in a Berlin museum, was exchanged for one owned by the Metropolitan. The pieces were assembled and the statue became whole once again after 3,400 years of dismemberment.

TOUR 2: Begin this tour on the second floor in Gallery 20 of the European Paintings Galleries. They are located upstairs and directly to the right of the Grand Staircase.

The European Paintings Collection includes 33 galleries displaying more than 1,000 masterpieces from the 13th through the late 19th centuries. You'll enjoy browsing through galleries hung with Spanish masterpieces by Goya and Velázquez, Italian Renaissance masters such as Raphael and Bronzino, Northern artists Dürer, Brueghel, and van Eyck, and Dutch masters Vermeer and Hals. There's also a world-class collection of Rembrandts. The following selections are among the author's favorites.

Francisco de Goya
Don Manuel Osorio Manrique de Zuniga, 1788 (Gallery 20)

This elegantly attired four-year-old boy was the son of the Spanish Count of Altamira. In his small hand he holds a string attached to a magpie, a favorite pet in the late 18th century. More birds rest in a cage on the floor, as two cats lurking in the background peer out hungrily at the magpie. Goya was particularly fond of doing children's portraits, perhaps because he had 19 of his own!

While this appears as a picture of sweet innocence, Goya may actually have intended it as a spiritual illustration—one showing the innocence of childhood confronting the forces of evil. He does this by borrowing symbolism from earlier times. In Renaissance painting, for example, the Christ Child (representing innocence) was often depicted with a bird

on a string and caged birds dupli-
cated this symbol during the baroque
era. As a counterbalance to the
theme of innocence, Goya portrays
menacing cats as the personification
of worldly evil.

Goya was Spain's premier artist in
the latter part of the 18th century,
and one of its most prolific. He
painted approximately 200 portraits
of famous people, and completed
some 500 paintings, along with hundreds of drawings and etchings. He
was celebrated as a painter of great
originality who had the ability to
express a wide range of emotions.

Rembrandt van Rijn
Aristotle with a Bust of Homer,
c. 1653 (Gallery 13)

The bearded and hatted Aristotle
rests his hand thoughtfully on a bust
of Homer, who lived about five centuries earlier. Aristotle's other hand
touches a golden chain given to him
by Alexander the Great, who is
depicted on the medallion hanging
from the chain. As is often the case
in Dutch painting, antiquity is suggested not by antique clothing, but
simply by outdated clothing: the shirt
is derived from Venetian painting of
previous centuries, and the apron is
merely Rembrandt's idea of Renaissance costume.

The essential meaning of the
painting is this: Aristotle contem-
plates the difference between worldly
and spiritual values, as represented
by the chain (honor and wealth) and
Homer (learning, literature) respec-
tively. The picture was commissioned
by Antonio Ruffo, a Sicilian noble-
man; it is dated 1653; it was later
bought by an English collector
around 1800.

Rembrandt van Rijn
Flora, c. 1655 (Gallery 13)

A pensive and pretty young woman
wearing a fancy flowered hat is
shown in three-quarter length profile.
The portrait is named for Flora, the
Roman goddess of spring and flowers. She resembles
Hendrickje Stoffels,
who became Rem-
brandt's companion
and the nurse of his
son Titus after his
first wife, Saskia, died
in 1642. Rembrandt's
interpretation is
unusual in that the
offering of flowers,
meaning love, is
accompanied by a
sense of sadness or
nostalgia, as if to
suggest Flora's aware-
ness that flowers,
youth, and love are
all short-lived.

Rembrandt, *Aristotle with a Bust of Homer*

Jan Vermeer
Young Woman with a Water Jug,
c. 1662 (Gallery 12)

This is typical of Vermeer's paintings: it shows a quiet Dutch interior with a young woman standing by a window. The basin and the pitcher were traditional symbols of purity, which Vermeer contrasts with the jewel box (luxury) on the table, and perhaps with the map (worldliness). The carefully balanced design of rectangles and other simple shapes, the primary colors, and the stillness of the light suggest tranquility or a state of harmony in domestic life. Vermeer was happily married and had several children at the time; and The Netherlands was flourishing, with the highest standard of living per capita in Europe.

It's a fact: *This canvas was the first Vermeer in America (1887); there were 13 by 1920, and there are 14 today. The Metropolitan Museum of Art has more than any other museum in the world (5), out of only 35 works known to exist today.*

What is a masterpiece?

Everyone is familiar with the word, but few know how and why the term originated. During the Middle Ages, the term "masterpiece" was associated with the apprentices who worked under the guidance of a "master" in a workshop. After years of training, when the apprentice achieved a certain level of excellence, he presented a work for entrance into the guild as a master; this was called a "masterpiece" and allowed him to conduct business on his own.

The concept of creating a masterpiece began to change in the 16th century when artists gained greater personal recognition. Also, aspiring artists began to learn their skills at art academies, which were institutions that were separate and distinct from the older, traditional guilds. Works of art were still required for admission to these academies, but they would not necessarily be classified as masterpieces.

Today, the term commonly refers to an outstanding work by an artist displaying the skill he or she has achieved in a particular medium. A masterpiece may stand out because of its subject matter, the way in which materials are used, the manner in which ideas are expressed, the artist's unique approach to technique, or any combination of the above. It also implies that there is a quality about the work, difficult to define exactly, that makes it hold up under the test of time.

Agnolo Bronzino
Portait of a Young Man, 1535–40
(Gallery 7)

This painting of a proud young member of the court of Cosimo I of Florence is one the Met's great masterpieces. Appearing sophisticated and elegant, the young man's long fingers caress a book, a reference to his intellectual pursuits. The other hand rests on his hip, emphasizing his long torso and gently arched back. He gazes directly out at the viewer, poised, haughty, and nonchalant.

This work is done in the Florentine "Mannerist" style made popular first by Michelangelo, and then by his followers, including Bronzino. Symbols and physical characteristics of people in Mannerist paintings share these similarities: small heads, long torsos, "mannered" gestures of the hands, a love for masks (see the appearance of one on the lower left), and an exquisitely smooth painting technique.

Lucas Cranach the Elder
Judgment of Paris, c. 1528
(Gallery 26)

The seated Paris is wearing a full set of armor and a feathered hat while Mercury is shown with a winged headdress. They appear to be conversing as the three goddesses Juno, Minerva, and Venus parade before them, wearing nothing more than their necklaces. A horse with a rose in its teeth peeks coyly around the tree trunk to leer at their smooth, slender, and elegant bodies. Meanwhile, Cupid, hovering in the sky above, prepares to shoot a love dart.

Cranach's *Judgment of Paris* refers to a myth from ancient times. According to legend, Paris was attending a friend's wedding when suddenly, Eris, the goddess of strife, threw down a golden apple that landed at his feet. He saw that it was inscribed with a message, "To the fairest," implying that Paris was to be the judge of the prettiest lady at the party. There were three goddesses who competed for the prize: Juno, who promised Paris wealth; Minerva, who promised Paris triumph in war; and Venus, who promised Paris the love of any woman he wanted, and described Helen of Troy as a possible choice. In the end, Paris chose Venus as the fairest maiden at the party and awarded her the golden apple. Paris promptly sailed for Troy in search of Helen, whom he eventually rescued from captivity.

Lucas Cranach the Elder was a popular artist in his time, as well as a successful businessman who served as an official in his native city of Wittemburg. He was well-known for his depictions of females, especially nudes, wearing large hats and jewelry, as shown in the *Judgment of Paris.* Cranach also created religious works. His son, Lucas Cranach the Younger, also became an artist. He emulated his father's style so well that it is difficult to distinguish between them.

Continue on to the Nineteenth-Century European Paintings and Sculpture Galleries.

Nineteenth-Century European Paintings and Sculpture Galleries—You enter through a light-filled gallery dominated by sculpture beyond which are numerous rooms hung with works by Renoir, Degas, Monet, van Gogh, and many of the other French Impressionists and Post-Impressionists. The following are some favorites.

Jean-Léon Gérôme
Pygmalion and Galatea, after 1861
(Sculpture Gallery)

This captivating painting shows an artist locked in an embrace with the nude statue of Galatea as she begins to metamorphose from stone into a living person.

The painting represents a legend, according to Ovid, about the King of Cypress who fell in love with a statue of Venus. The king carved a likeness of her to keep as his own, and prayed to the goddess that he might be rewarded with a wife as beautiful as she. Venus heard his prayers and was so impressed with his sincerity that she brought the statue to life as a favor to the lovesick king. The statue eventually became known as Galatea.

Artists liked to portray the moment of transformation in a setting suggesting an atelier. As you can see, Gérôme, in keeping with this tradition, has placed the couple in an artist's studio surrounded by sculptor's tools, carved busts, paints, and palette.

Camille Pissarro
The Boulevard Montmartre on a Winter Morning, 1897

Horse-drawn carriages slog along a busy boulevard past long rows of buildings. The street is alive with people and activity—gentlemen in overcoats and ladies bundled against the cold—leaving no doubt that it's a frigid winter day. Even the trees are stripped of leaves, adding to the sense of extreme cold. Pissarro used the view from his window in the Grand Hotel de Russie to paint this charming street scene. This is one of twelve paintings he did from this vantage point in every season of the year.

Pierre-Auguste Renoir
By the Seashore, 1883

Much of Renoir's appeal comes from his ability to paint beautiful women in relaxed settings. Here he creates a soft and lovely vision of a young lady in a wicker chair. Her pretty blue eyes engage the viewer as though caught slightly by surprise. In the distance is a sketchy view of the seashore.

Pierre-Auguste Renoir
Madame Charpentier and
Her Children, 1878

Most society portrait painters of the time would have placed their subjects in a more formal setting, perhaps in front of satin drapery or standing together in an elegant room. Instead, the innovative Renoir captures the young family in a more casual moment. Madame Charpentier, in an elegant black gown, leans leisurely against a floral sofa. Her daughter, Georgette, plops down on a large shaggy dog, while her younger brother, Paul (also in a dress), sits at his mother's side. The room is informally furnished with bamboo furniture and a woven carpet on the floor. The family pet, looking a bit doleful, adds a homey touch to this charming interior.

Madame Charpentier and her husband were a well-established and influential Parisian couple. He was the publisher for Zola and Flaubert, and she was known for hosting literary and political salons.

Édouard Manet
Woman with a Parrot, 1866

In Manet's time it was common for women to have parrots as pets. Their intelligence and their absolute devotion to their owners were considered admirable qualities. And, after all, one could divulge secrets to a parrot and never have them repeated.

Manet presents a woman holding a monocle while standing in a pink robe. As her parrot sips water from a container, she savors the sweet smell of a bouquet of violets.

Renoir, *Madame Charpentier and Her Children*

It has been suggested that in this painting Manet was spoofing the theme of the five senses often favored by 17th-century Dutch artists. If so, every object has a hidden meaning, with the monocle representing sight, the parrot and the water representing hearing and taste, and the violets representing smell and touch. There's also an orange peel on the base of the perch that may represent the passage of time, the loss of the senses, and death. Such themes were repeated over and over in Dutch *vanitas* paintings.

Claude Monet
Rouen Cathedral: The Portal
(*in sun*), 1894

Rouen Cathedral was a subject Monet painted over and over again at various times of the day and in all kinds of weather. He was able to demonstrate how the elements and the quality of light upon the surface of a building could change the mood of a painting. This particular view of the cathedral was painted at noon on a sunny day.

Monet created over 30 paintings of Rouen Cathedral, this being one of a series of 18 that were shown at a Paris exhibition in 1895.

Continue on to the Ancient Near Eastern Art Galleries.
Some of the oldest works of art in the Metropolitan's collection are to be found in the Ancient Near Eastern Art Galleries. There are significant remnants of ancient civilizations that geographically cover an area from Turkey to Pakistan. Many are colossal in size, and others are so diminutive that you must look carefully to find them. The following works are two of the most famous in this collection.

Winged Human-Headed Lions, Assyria, 883-859 B.C.

Colossal in size and carved from limestone, these figures stand over ten feet high and originally served as guardian spirits in the palace of King Ashurnasirpal II at Nimrud. Notice that they have five legs!

The Pacing Lion, Babylon, 604–562 B.C.

This is a section of a large wall piece taken from the Processional Way of King Nebuchadnezzar II's Palace. Individual portions of the lion's body were carefully molded and fitted together like a giant puzzle. Made from blue glazed and natural brick, it's a superb example of the quality of craftsmanship from this era.

Illustrations

p. 44: Metropolitan Museum of Art, Exterior

p. 49: *Armor of George Clifford, 3rd Earl of Cumberland,* circa 1590. Gilded steel, brass, and leather. 69$\frac{1}{2}$″ high (176.5 cm). Rogers Fund, 32.130.6 a-y, The Metropolitan Museum of Art.

p. 50: Metropolitan Museum of Art, American Wing Garden Court (interior shot)

p. 51: *Frank Lloyd Wright Room,* Living room from the Little House, Wayzata, Minnesota, 1912–15. H. 13 ft. 8 in. (4.17 m), L. 46 ft. (14 m), W. 28 ft. (8.53 m). Purchase, Emily B. Chadbourne Bequest, 1972, 1972.60.1, The Metropolitan Museum of Art.

p. 52: John Singer Sargent, *Madame X (Madame Pierre Gautreau),* 1884. Oil on canvas. 82$\frac{1}{8}$″ × 43$\frac{1}{4}$″ (208.6 × 109.9 cm). Purchase, Arthur Hoppock Hearn Fund, 1916, 16.53, The Metropolitan Museum of Art.

p. 53: Emanuel Leutze, *Washington Crossing the Delaware,* 1851. Oil on canvas. 149″ × 255″ (378.5 × 647.7 cm). Gift of John S. Kennedy, 1897, 97.34, The Metropolitan Museum of Art.

p. 55: *Outer Coffin of Henettaway,* Thebes, Deir al Bahri, Dynasty 21, circa 1039–992 B.C. Gessoed and painted wood. 79$\frac{7}{8}$ inches long (203 cm). Rogers Fund, 1925, 25.3.182, The Metropolitan Museum of Art.

p. 56: Francisco Goya, *Don Manuel Osorio Manrique de Zuniga,* 1788. Oil on canvas. 50″ × 40″ (127 × 121.6 cm). The Jules Bache Fund, 1949, 49.7.41, The Metropolitan Museum of Art.

p. 57: Rembrandt van Rijn, *Aristotle with a Bust of Homer,* 1653. Oil on canvas. 56$\frac{1}{2}$″ × 53$\frac{3}{4}$″ (143.5 × 136.5 cm). Purchase, Funds from Friends of the Museum, 1961, 61.198, The Metropolitan Museum of Art.

p. 58: Johannes Vermeer, *Young Woman with a Water Jug,* circa 1662. Oil on canvas. 18″ × 16″ (45.7 × 40.6 cm). Gift of Henry Marquand, 1889, Marquand Collection, 89.15.21, The Metropolitan Museum of Art.

p. 60: Camille Pissarro, *The Boulevard Montmartre on a Winter Morning,* 1897. Oil on canvas. 25½″ × 32″. Gift of Katrin S. Vietor, in loving memory of Ernest G. Vietor, 1960, 60.174, The Metropolitan Museum of Art.

p. 61: Auguste Renoir, *Madame Charpentier and Her Children,* 1878. Oil on canvas. 50½″ × 74⅞″ (153.7 × 190.2 cm). Wolfe Fund, 1907. Catherine Lorillard Wolfe Collection, 07.122, The Metropolitan Museum of Art.

The Museum of Modern Art

Jacob Lawrence
THE MIGRATION SERIES

MoMA

Kandinsky Compositions

Address:
11 West 53rd Street
(between 5th and 6th Avenues)
(Midtown Manhattan, West Side)
New York, New York 10019
(212) 708-9480

Hours:
Open: Saturday–Tuesday 10:30–6;
         Thursday, Friday 10:30–8:30
Closed: Wednesday

Entry Fees:
Yes. Children under 16 free if with
an adult.

Type:
Art

Transportation:
Subway: E, F to 5th Avenue/
         53rd Street
Bus: M1, M2, M3, M4, M5
         to 53rd Street

Museum Shop:
Yes. The Museum Shop, adjacent to
the main lobby, offers books, posters,
cards, and gifts. MoMA Design Store,
located across the street at 44 West
53rd sells design objects, furniture,
gadgets, and miscellaneous gift items.

Restaurant:
Yes

Disabled Access:
Yes; wheelchairs available
at coat-check area

Lower Floor

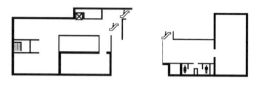

Ground Floor

The Abby Aldrich Rockefeller Sculpture Garden
Matisse "Backs I–IV"
Picasso "She-Goat"
Nadelman "Man in the Open Air"
Lachaise "Standing Woman"

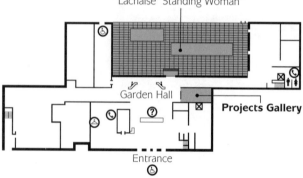

Garden Hall

Projects Gallery

Entrance

2nd Floor

Post-Impressionism
Rousseau, Cézanne,
van Gogh

Picasso
"Demoiselles
d'Avignon"

Surrealism
Dali, Magritte

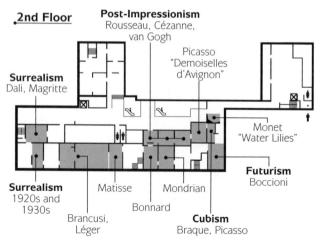

Monet
"Water Lilies"

Surrealism
1920s and
1930s

Matisse

Brancusi,
Léger

Bonnard

Mondrian

Cubism
Braque, Picasso

Futurism
Boccioni

3rd Floor

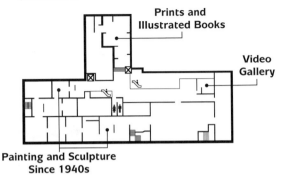

Prints and
Illustrated Books

Video
Gallery

Painting and Sculpture
Since 1940s

4th Floor

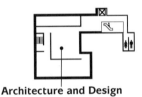

Architecture and Design

*This floor plan highlights only the areas included in the suggested tour.
A detailed floor plan of the museum is available at the Information Desk.*

What to Expect

The Museum of Modern Art occupies the lower floors of a Midtown Manhattan skyscraper built around a sculpture garden. Assembled under its roof, available to one and all, are the highest achievements of every major artist of the 20th century.

The collections begin with Post-Impressionist masters from the 1880s and progress through the entire 20th century, with virtually every movement in modern European and American art represented. Paintings and sculpture including celebrated works such as van Gogh's *Starry Night,* Rousseau's *The Sleeping Gypsy,* Picasso's landmark *Les Demoiselles d'Avignon,* and Dali's strange *Persistence of Memory.* Other galleries, reached by escalators that rise through the light-filled glass Garden Hall, feature photography, architectural models, design objects, drawings and prints, and illustrated books. MoMA also has two theaters that feature films every day from the Museum's comprehensive collection of more than 10,000 movies and videos.

Plan to visit the charming Abby Aldrich Rockefeller Sculpture Garden where, among fountains and trees, you'll discover Picasso's whimsical *She-Goat,* Elie Nadelman's jaunty *Man in the Open Air,* Matisse's well-known series, *Backs I–IV,* and numerous other distinctive 20th-century sculptures.

Expect to come upon one of MoMA's highly acclaimed special exhibitions that showcase the works of well-known artists. And, when you're ready for a break, there's casual cafe-style dining in the Garden Cafe, and elegant dining in the Museum's new restaurant, Sette MoMA.

Special Information

- Gallery talks and slide presentations weekdays.
- Special talks for hearing impaired.
- Sculpture touch tours for visually impaired visitors.
- Special art and sculpture exhibitions.
- Film and video showings.
- Call (212) 708-9480 for current schedule of activities.

> ### Suggested 60-Minute Tour
> *Concentrate on the second floor galleries and the Abby Aldrich Rockefeller Sculpture Garden. Begin at the top of the escalator in Gallery 2.*

Highlights

✳ Vincent van Gogh
Starry Night, 1889 (Gallery 2)

✳ Henri Rousseau
The Sleeping Gypsy, 1897
(Gallery 3)

Van Gogh's vision of a night sky, with its swirling, flickering stars, courses forward like waves of a rolling surf. Flame-like cypress trees pierce the upper vortex and in the distance a small town nestles in darkness. The turbulence is accentuated by thickly applied pigments of deep blues, greens, and yellows. Every slashing brushstroke seems to emit a torrent of anguished emotion; every object has its own direction and rhythm which emphasizes the contours of the land and sky.

Starry Night was painted in June 1889 at Saint-Remy after the artist underwent a period of crisis and religious hallucinations. Van Gogh's output was enormous during the last two years of his life, with an astonishing production of hundreds of paintings that are today considered masterpieces. He died in 1890 of a self-inflicted gunshot wound to the head at the age of 37.

Rousseau demonstrates his great imaginative powers in the celebrated *Sleeping Gypsy*, one of MoMA's most popular paintings. He portrays a gypsy lady resting peacefully beside her mandolin and water jar. A lion lowers its head as if to nudge the slumbering woman while the moon hovers above. The picture, set in a silent dream-like desert, takes on an aura of haunting beauty and mystery. Rousseau claimed that this painting was inspired by a trip he made to Mexico while serving in the French army. The story was fabricated, however, and in reality his sources came from books and visits to the Paris zoo and botanical gardens.

Rousseau was an untrained amateur painter who worked as a customs collector in Paris. He endured a lifetime of rejection and ridicule by his peers and died a pauper in 1910, never having achieved success and recognition for his work. In the years following his death, however, scorn gave way to admiration by artists and critics alike, and today his paintings are considered masterpieces.

Pablo Picasso
Les Demoiselles d'Avignon,
1906–07 (Gallery 4)

The subjects of Picasso's large painting are prostitutes who worked in a Barcelona brothel familiar to the artist. The title, translated as "The Girls of Avignon," was a joking reference to the Carrer d'Avinyo (Avignon Street), where the house of ill repute was located in Barcelona.

Early studies for the painting show that the artist initially intended it as a moralistic message. In the center was a sailor holding a wineglass surrounded by the nude women, and to the left was a medical student who presumably administered treatment for venereal disease. Picasso later brushed these figures out of the final work, leaving only the women. Their various stances were adapted from classical Greek and Roman sculpture, ancient Iberian figures, and African masks he'd seen in a Paris exhibition. Their figure styles become more fragmented, moving from poses assumed by classical sculpture, on the left, to increasingly distorted figures on the right.

Demoiselles is considered a landmark work because it shows evidence of Picasso's struggle toward a new style: each figure is a nontraditional angular shape; the African-looking masks of the faces on the right are a departure from traditional representations;

masses are flattened; and there is no attempt to reconstruct on canvas the use of three-dimensional perspective.

When *Demoiselles* was first exhibited, Picasso's fellow artists considered it incomprehensible. Today, it is no longer considered shocking; rather, it is viewed as a turning point in his career, the precursor of Cubism, which he developed in collaboration with Georges Braque between 1907 and 1914.

Pablo Picasso
Ma Jolie, 1911 (Gallery 5)

A look at two representative "analytical" paintings by Braque and Picasso will help to clarify the aim of the cubists. In *Ma Jolie,* Picasso presents

Picasso, *Ma Jolie*

a female figure with a guitar as seen from a variety of simultaneously staged viewpoints. At the top of the painting a network of horizontal and vertical lines configure a woman's head; an angled left arm, hand, and fingers can be discerned on the lower right; and in the center are the vertical strings of a guitar. The printed treble clef and musical staff on the lower right make reference to the musical instrument.

Don't worry if you have trouble seeing the disparate parts on your first try. It takes a practiced eye to put it all together.

The title, *Ma Jolie,* has a double meaning: it stems from the title of a song that was popular in Picasso's day, and it was also a pet name for his lover, Eva Gouel.

Georges Braque
Man with a Guitar, 1911–12
(Gallery 5)

Now look closely at Braque's *Man With a Guitar* (which usually hangs alongside Picasso's *Ma Jolie*), and you'll be able to make out some striking similarities between the two. As in Picasso's painting, Braque's color scheme is made up of dark greens, grays, and blacks. The shapes are scattered without reference to traditional proportion. And it, too, is a portrait of a guitar player. Shown at the top is the musician's profile. His right arm is long, bent at the elbow; alongside are fragments of keys, strings, and other instrument parts.

It's not surprising that these paintings are so similar, for Braque and Picasso worked closely to form a new kind of representational art. The two young artists often compared

their work and discussed their progress, which ultimately led to the full-blown development of Cubism.

Throughout his lifetime Picasso worked in a constellation of styles including Cubism. Braque's work, on the other hand, took a different course. Following a serious injury suffered during World War I, he abandoned his interest in cubist theories and his work became less angular and more gracefully rounded. He concentrated on producing still life paintings, book illustrations, stage sets, costume designs, and decorative work.

Cubism is an art movement developed by Georges Braque and Pablo Picasso between 1907 and 1914. They revolutionized the time-honored precepts that art should imitate nature, that representations of figures or objects must be "real," and that they should be shown from a fixed viewpoint. Instead, Cubism shows the subject simultaneously from several viewpoints, making it appear multifaceted. "Analytical Cubism" refers to the developmental phase, up to 1912, characterized by geometric structures and muted dark colors. This was followed by "Synthetic Cubism" in which colors became stronger, shapes more decorative, and elements such as strips of newsprint and stencilling were incorporated into the paintings. Cubism had a profound influence on all later movements of abstract art in the 20th century.

Umberto Boccioni
*Unique Forms of Continuity
in Space*, 1913 (bronze)
(Gallery 7)

Poised on two blocks of unequal size,
Boccioni portrays a striding human
figure that has been grotesquely
distorted by speed and wind. Arms,
legs, and torso appear blown into a
mass of rippling bronze, creating an
overall effect of extreme movement
and agitation.

Inspiration for this dynamic work
of art came out of Boccioni's association with the Futurists, an organization established in 1909 by the Italian
poet Filippo Marinetti. Its members
were artists who were fascinated by
the machine age and extolled the
values of industrial civilization. They
advocated the production of paintings and sculpture that represented
time and movement. Cars, trains, and
later, airplanes became their favorite
subjects because they stood for qualities associated with speed, power,
energy, and boldness. For Boccioni,
Unique Forms of Continuity in Space
was the artistic summation of these
qualities.

None of Boccioni's sculptures
were cast in his lifetime, and most of
his working plasters were destroyed
in a fire in Milan, following a posthu-
mous exhibition. Fragments, including
Unique Forms of Continuity in Space,
were lovingly collected and reconstructed by Marinetti and his friends
and eventually cast in bronze. Most
of his work is known to us only
through photographs. Boccioni's
brilliant career ended in 1916 due
to an accident while serving in the
Italian army.

Piet Mondrian
Broadway Boogie Woogie, 1943
(Gallery 10)

Broadway Boogie Woogie,
Mondrian's distinctive geometric
abstraction, is made up of simplified
grids that incorporate primary colors
plus black, white, and gray. The title
refers both to the energetic pulse of
the large American city and his love
of jazz music.

Mondrian's paintings are reduced
to the bare essentials, absolutely
devoid of realistic representations,
optical perspective, the curved line,
and texture.

Mondrian used a shortcut,
learned in America, to produce this
painting. Strips of adhesive tape were
laid on the canvas to configure the
composition and then were removed
once the paint had been applied.

Mondrian's works have had a profound influence on advertising art,
decorative art, and industrial design.
This was his last completed work,
painted in New York City.

Pierre Bonnard
The Breakfast Room, 1930–31
(Gallery 11)

Bonnard creates three separate areas
of interest in this highly colorful composition. In the foreground is a view
of a dining area complete with table
settings, teapot, fruits, and other
objects. The window opens onto a
veranda, and beyond that is a lush
garden. The striped tablecloth, the
tall rectangular window, and the
clever use of color pulls the eye
deeper and deeper into the picture.

Notice how the colors of objects in the background are much more subdued than those inside, giving the illusion of distance.

Bonnard worked as a graphic artist and studied in Paris at the Ecole des Beaux-Arts. He exhibited regularly at the Salon des Independents and in 1903 helped establish the Salon d'Automne organized by the Fauves.

As a young artist, Bonnard was influenced by Gauguin's use of strong colors and patterns. He also adapted the lyrical elements of Impressionism and Pointillism to his quiet scenes which have come to be termed "intimist."

Henri Matisse
The Red Studio, 1911 (Gallery 12)

The subject of this painting is Matisse's studio. In it he places a selection of his own art including pictures, sculptures, ceramics, and other personal belongings. All of the objects appear to float within a brilliant red room. Softly outlined is a grandfather clock, a chest of drawers, and pedestals for pieces of sculpture. Upon the table in the foreground is a ceramic plate of his design, a wineglass, and a vase with a trailing vine. Against the walls, in miniature scale, are several of his paintings including *Nude with White Scarf* (1909), and *Large Nude with Necklace*.

Henri Matisse
Dance (I), 1909 (Gallery 12)

Dance (I) portrays female nudes dancing in a circle set against areas of green and blue. Their flattened shapes are defined with only a few simple lines. All of the figures are equal in size and any measure of perspective or depth has been eliminated. The utter simplicity of the composition and exuberant use of color radiates a sense of freedom and pleasure.

Inspiration for the dance theme came to Matisse one day in 1905 while vacationing near the Spanish border. When he saw a group of Catalan fishermen dancing in a circle on the beach, the visual impact so stirred his imagination that he soon began to incorporate a ring of dancers into his paintings.

Matisse's first masterpiece on this theme was a composition produced in 1905–06 which he called *The Joy of Life* (owned by the Barnes Foundation, Merion, Pennsylvania). Then in 1909 Sergei Shchukin, a wealthy Russian businessman-collector and Matisse's patron, asked him to produce some paintings on the same theme for his house in Moscow. MoMA's *Dance (I)* was made as a study for this project.

Two more paintings, *Dance (II)*, a more violently colored rendition of the dance, and *Music,* eventually were bought by Shchukin, who hung them in his stairway. Today those paintings remain in Russia in the Hermitage collection.

Fernand Léger
Three Women, 1921 (Gallery 13)

Following World War I, Léger joined a movement in French painting called Purism, which exemplified an anti-emotional "machine aesthetic." A major work from this period is his monumental *Three Women*, which expresses Léger's fascination with the relationship between man and the machine age. The figures appear as highly polished robots that have been reduced to static geometrically simplified forms. The furniture upon which they rest is made up of a series of cylinders, giving a hint of machinery design. All objects in the room are also geometrically shaped and even though the table laden with food implies sociability, there's little to suggest that there is anything real or personal in this mechanical environment.

At the beginning of his career Léger was a major figure in the development of Cubism. When he moved to Paris in 1900 he worked as an architectural draftsman and studied art part-time at the Ecole des Beaux-Arts. By 1911 he had become a leading collaborator in the Cubist movement, using fragmented tubular forms and bright colors offset by white tones as his signature style. MoMA owns several of his paintings from this era including the large *Exit the Ballet Russes* (1914) which is usually on display and would be well worth looking at for comparison.

Constantin Brancusi
Bird in Space, c. 1927 (bronze)
(Gallery 13)

This elegant abstraction of a bird in flight is one of Brancusi's most recognized works. His simplified form captures the essence of a bird rising upward through space. To add to the illusion, he has polished the bronze to a shiny finish in order to convey a sense of speed. The sculpture, placed on a two-part geometrically shaped pedestal made of textured stone, contrasts dramatically with the smooth, organic form of the bird.

Brancusi, a Romanian by birth, migrated to Paris where he did most of his work. He enrolled in the Ecole des Beaux-Arts in 1904 and later worked as Rodin's assistant. He soon left to strike out on his own, declaring, "Nothing can grow in the shadow of a giant tree." Brancusi worked in marble, bronze, and wood, and created many pedestals in these materials which he occasionally exhibited as individual works of art. His greatest achievement, however, was his ability to reduce complex natural forms into abstract simplicity.

René Magritte
The False Mirror (Le Faux Miroir),
1929 (Gallery 16)

Magritte, the famous Belgian
Surrealist, is best known for using
commonplace objects in ambiguous
and often disquieting ways. In *The
False Mirror,* one of his most thought-
provoking paintings, Magritte tempts
the viewer into believing that the
eye's surface is a mirror, reflecting a
blue sky with clouds drifting through
it. He retains the pupil, however, perhaps as a reminder that it really *is* an
eye. The painting is confusing because
it combines coherent recognition with
irrational representation.

Salvador Dali
The Persistence of Memory, 1931
(Gallery 16)

Dali confronts the viewer immediately
with his images of melting, oozing
watches that stretch across odd sur-
faces—a barren tree branch, a block
of stone, and a biomorphic blob, said
to be a profile of the artist with his
nose pointing down. On this deso-
late beach, with rocky cliffs in the
distance, everything appears dead
except the ants and a fly that attack
the inorganic watches. It's difficult to
imagine any landscape as baffling as
this one.

The Persistence of Memory is recognized as one of the most irrational
Surrealist paintings of the 20th century, and one of the most famous.

Surrealism *was a movement in
art and literature that originated
in France and spread throughout
the art world especially during
the 1920s and 1930s. The
Surrealist group was started in
1924 in Paris by André Breton,
a writer and critic. Within the
group were anti-war activists
from the earlier Dada movement and other artists and
intellectuals.*

*Feelings of despair, the advent
of psychoanalysis, and the hor-
rors of World War I were the
main influences for Surrealist
art. Sigmund Freud's theories
about the subconscious also
had a significant influence on
the Surrealist movement.*

*In its most popular form it is
characterized by a preoccupation
with the bizarre and the irrational, often using thoughts
buried in the unconscious mind
and the odd juxtaposition of
unrelated objects. Nightmares
and other hallucinatory images,
painted in a precise realistic
style, mix with reality in odd
ways. Salvador Dali's "Persistence of Memory" is a good
example of this phenomenon
with its softened timepieces
slithering over tree branches.*

Claude Monet
Water Lilies, c. 1920
(Monet Gallery)

Monet's water gardens were created from a marshland on the artist's property in Giverny. He diverted a small branch of the River Epte to form a pond and then planted it with his beloved water lilies. A studio was constructed at one end that was large enough to hold his huge canvases. This became Monet's favorite retreat and served as a place of solitude and inspiration for much of his later work.

The soft blurred shapes of the water lilies show nuances of color and light as they float gently across three giant canvases. Vegetation barely appears beneath hazy blue and green water. The overall effect is one of quiet serenity.

Selections from the Abby Aldrich Rockefeller Sculpture Garden

All of the works listed below are usually found in the Abby Aldrich Rockefeller Sculpture Garden. However, during the winter months, the garden is usually closed to visitors, so you'll need to check with Information to find out where sculptures have been relocated.

Elie Nadelman
Man in the Open Air, 1915

One of Nadelman's best-known works is this interpretation of a jaunty, bow-tied, bowler-hatted man that captures the essence of a gentleman dandy. Its extraordinarily simplified form exudes an air of nonchalance.

Nadelman came to New York from Poland in 1914 to further his career as an artist. Not long after his arrival he was commissioned by Helena Rubinstein to sculpt sleek marble heads which were placed in her salons. He met and married a wealthy New York widow, which may account for the fact that his work has a witty sophistication appropriate to the high-society world in which he moved. Nadelman's career came to an end in 1935 following the accidental destruction of much of his work.

Pablo Picasso
She-Goat, 1950, cast 1952

Picasso's innovative spirit is evident in his whimsical version of a goat. Look closely and you'll see that it is an assemblage of familiar objects: the spine is a palm leaf, the ribs are wicker baskets, and the udders are pottery jugs.

Picasso created a variety of animals in all media during his long career as an artist. His imagination allowed him to "see" and fashion animals from bits and pieces of everyday objects. He is well-known for his paintings and sculptures of bulls, birds of all varieties, baboons, cats, and dogs, many of which were his own pets.

Henri Matisse
Backs I–IV, 1909–1929
(against the far wall)

Backs I–IV demonstrate how, over a period of 20 years, Matisse's ideas about the human figure underwent a remarkable transition.

You can see that *Back I,* cast in 1909, is a reasonable representation of the back of a female nude. The buttocks are well-defined, the muscles of her back ripple, and an anatomically realistic breast protrudes under the raised arm. *Back II* and *Back III* quickly followed each other

in 1913 and 1914 and show increased abstaction and simplification of the anatomy.

In *Back IV,* the last of the series, the body is now broken up into two large masses, separated by the nude's head and a pointed rope of hair that dangles down her back. This work demonstrates how Matisse, over a period of 20 years, has made a complete transition from a traditional representation of human anatomy to a remarkable simplification of form.

Gaston Lachaise
Standing Woman, 1912–18

Measuring over six and a half feet tall, *Standing Woman* exudes a sense of powerful overt sexuality. She rises rhythmically from delicately poised feet to curvaceous hips and back into a slender waist that swells again into broad shoulders and bent arms.

When Lachaise first exhibited the clay model for *Standing Woman* in New York City in 1918, it was termed grotesque, fat, and an insult to the American ideal of slender femininity. It has since become a well-regarded icon of American sculpture.

French-born, but active most of his life in the United States, Lachaise emigrated to Boston then moved to New York City where he was an assistant to Paul Manship. He drew inspiration from the sculpture of all cultures, particularly fertility goddesses and the erotic sculpture of India and the Malay peninsula. Lachaise is considered one of the great pioneers of modern sculpture.

Museum of Modern Art, interior of gallery

Illustrations

p. 66: Museum of Modern Art, exterior

p. 71: (left) Vincent van Gogh, *Starry Night,* 1889. Oil on canvas. 29 × 36¼" (73 × 92.1 cm). The Museum of Modern Art, New York. Acquired through the Lillie P. Bliss Bequest. Photograph © 1996 The Museum of Modern Art, New York.

p. 71: (right) Henri Rousseau, *The Sleeping Gypsy,* 1897. 51" × 6'7" (129 × 200.7 cm). Oil on canvas. The Museum of Modern Art, New York. Gift of Mrs. Simon Guggenheim. Photograph © 1996 The Museum of Modern Art, New York.

p. 72: Pablo Picasso, *Ma Jolie* (winter 1911–1912). Oil on canvas, 39³⁄₈" × 25³⁄₄" (100 × 65.4 cm). The Museum of Modern Art, New York. Acquired through the Lillie P. Bliss Bequest. Photograph © 1996 The Museum of Modern Art, New York.

p. 75: Henri Matisse, *Dance I* (first version), Paris, 1909. Oil on canvas. 8'6½" × 12'9½" (259.7 × 390.1 cm). The Museum of Modern Art, New York. The gift of Nelson A. Rockefeller in honor of Alfred H. Barr, Jr. Photograph © 1996 The Museum of Modern Art, New York.

p. 76: Fernand Léger, *Three Women* (*Le Grand Déjeuner*), 1921. Oil on canvas. 6'¼" × 8'3" (183.5 × 251.5 cm). The Museum of Modern Art, New York. Mrs. Simon Guggenheim Fund. Photograph © 1996 The Museum of Modern Art, New York.

p. 77: (top) René Magritte, *The False Mirror,* 1928. Oil on canvas. 21¼″ × 31⅞″ (54 × 80.9 cm). The Museum of Modern Art, New York. Purchase. Photograph © 1996 The Museum of Modern Art, New York.

p. 77: (bottom) Salvador Dali, *The Persistence of Memory (Persistance de la memoire*), 1931. Oil on canvas. 9½″ × 13″ (24.1 × 33 cm). The Museum of Modern Art, New York. Given anonymously. Photograph © 1996 The Museum of Modern Art, New York.

p. 78: Elie Nadelman, *Man in the Open Air,* ca. 1915. Bronze, 54½″ (138.4 cm high), at base 11¾″ × 21½″ (29.9 × 54.5 cm). The Museum of Modern Art, New York. Gift of William S. Paley (by exchange). Photograph © 1996 The Museum of Modern Art, New York.

p. 79: Pablo Picasso, *She-Goat (Vallauris*), 1950. Bronze. 46⅜″ × 28⅛″ (117.7 × 143.1 cm), including base. The Museum of Modern Art, New York. Mrs. Simon Guggenheim Fund. Photograph © 1996 The Museum of Modern Art, New York.

p. 80: Museum of Modern Art, interior of gallery

Part II:

General Directory

Museums That Showcase Art, History, and World Cultures

American Academy of Arts and Letters (Manhattan, Washington Heights)

Audubon Terrace, Broadway at 155th Street
New York, New York 10032-7599
(212) 368-5900

Open: Tuesday–Sunday (during exhibitions only) 1–4

Closed: Monday

Entry fees: Free

Type: The Arts

Subway: 1 train (not 9) to 157th Street and Broadway or B train to 155th Street and St. Nicholas Avenue. Walk west on 155th Street to Broadway and north one-half block on Broadway to Audubon Terrace.

Bus: 4, 5 north and south, stops at Broadway and 155th or 157th Street

Museum Shop: No

Restaurant: No

Disabled Access: Call ahead

The American Academy of Arts and Letters is an organization that pays tribute to distinguished writers, composers, musicians, artists, and architects. Members are elected to the Academy, an honor considered the highest formal recognition of artistic merit in America. Affiliates, past and present, include such figures as Mark Twain, Henry James, E. M. Forster, Childe Hassam, Agnes deMille, Richard Rodgers, Stephen Sondheim, Kurt Vonnegut, E. L. Doctorow, and two former American presidents, Woodrow Wilson and Theodore Roosevelt, both chosen for membership on the basis of their literary works.

The three exhibitions that are held each year feature works of art by candidates for awards (in March); works by newly elected members and award recipients (in May–June); and paintings by artists whose work is being considered for purchase and donation to museums (in November). Galleries are open to the public only during these periods. Visitors are asked to call ahead for current information.

American Craft Museum (Midtown Manhattan, West Side)

40 West 53rd Street (between 5th Avenue and Avenue of the Americas, across from Museum of Modern Art)
New York, New York 10019-6136
(212) 956-3535

Open: Tuesday 10–8; Wednesday–Sunday 10–5

Closed: Monday, major holidays

Entry fees: Yes

Type: Art, crafts

Subway: 1, 9 to 50th Street; N, R to 49th Street; E, F to Fifth Avenue

Bus: M1, M2, M3, M4, M5, M6, M7, M27, M30, M50, M57, M58, Q32

Museum Shop: Yes. Open museum hours and also Monday

Restaurant: No

Disabled Access: Yes

Enter a light-filled foyer and descend a dramatic staircase into galleries that display the very best in craft media. Exhibitions are always a surprise, with most featuring imaginatively designed functional items like furniture, clothing, plates, glassware, baskets, tapestries, rugs, and more. You'll be happy you stopped by.

The Asia Society Galleries (Manhattan, Upper East Side)

725 Park Avenue at 70th Street
New York, New York 10021
(212) 517-ASIA
(212) 517-NEWS
(current information)

Open: Tuesday–Saturday 11–6; Thursday 11–8; Sunday 12–5

Closed: Monday, major holidays

Entry fees: Yes

Type: Art, culture and contemporary affairs of Asia

Subway: Lexington Avenue line 6 to 68th Street and Hunter College

Bus: M1, M2, M3, M4, M30, M72 to Madison and 70th; M101, M102 to Lexington and 70th; M30, M72 to Park and 72nd; M66 to Park and 67th or 68th

Museum Shop: Yes

Restaurant: No

Disabled Access: Yes

Learn about the arts, history, culture, and current affairs of Asia through a variety of ongoing art exhibitions, lectures, seminars, conferences, and educational programs. Countries represented in its permanent collection include China, India, Korea, Indonesia, and Cambodia. Art exhibitions are on display throughout the year. Recent shows have highlighted the traditional and contemporary arts of Asia and selections from the Society's permanent collection, the Mr. and Mrs. John D. Rockefeller III Collection of Asian Art.

The Bronx Museum of the Arts (Bronx)

1040 Grand Concourse
at East 165th Street
Bronx, New York 10456-3999
(718) 681-6000

Open: Wednesday 3–9; Thursday and Friday 10–5; Saturday–Sunday 1–6

Closed: Monday, Tuesday

Entry fees: Yes. Suggested donation

Type: Art, contemporary life

Subway: D to 161st Street/Yankee Stadium; D to 167th Street (9:30–3:30 only), 4 to 161st Street

Bus: BX1 or BX2 to 165th Street and Grand Concourse

Museum Shop: Yes

Restaurant: No

Disabled Access: Yes

The Bronx Museum of the Arts, one of the most respected art museums outside of Manhattan, offers changing exhibitions focusing on art of the 20th century and subjects relating to the cultural diversity of the Bronx. Its permanent collection encompasses the geographical areas of Africa, Latin America, and Southeast Asia as well as the American descendants of these areas.

The museum also sponsors educational programs including performing arts events, lectures, and panel discussions. Year-round classes are offered to children and adults in art and media studies as well as interpretive gallery tours for schools and special interest groups.

Brooklyn Historical Society (Brooklyn)

128 Pierrepont Street (corner of Pierrepont and Clinton Streets)
Brooklyn, New York 11201
(718) 624-0890

Open: Tuesday–Saturday, 12–5

Closed: Sunday, Monday

Entry fees: Yes. Free on Wednesday

Type: History

Subway: Close to all major subway lines. 2, 3, 4, or 5 to Borough Hall; M, N, or R to Court Street; or the A, C, or F to Jay Street/Borough Hall

Bus: Use buses that stop near Borough Hall: B25, B26, B37, B41, B45, B52, B61

Museum Shop: No

Restaurant: No

Disabled Access: Yes

The museum presents exhibitions and programs that focus on urban life in Brooklyn, its people, its cultural diversity, its neighborhoods and its industries past and present. There's also an excellent library where you can research all aspects of life in this famous borough. Highlights from the permanent collection are organized around five familiar symbols of Brooklyn: the Brooklyn Bridge, Coney Island, Brooklynites, the Brooklyn Navy Yard, and the Brooklyn Dodgers. Outstanding attractions include the enormous eagle sculpture that once stood atop the *Brooklyn Daily Eagle* building, the Brooklyn Bridge Construction Wheel, *The Honeymooners* stage set, a wax museum, and Brooklyn Dodgers' memorabilia.

The Brooklyn Museum (Brooklyn, Prospect Heights)

See pages 18–34 for detailed information.

Castle Clinton National Monument (Lower Manhattan)

Battery Park
New York, New York
(212) 344-7220

Open: Daily 8:30–4:30

Closed: Christmas, New Year's Day

Subway: 4, 5 to Bowling Green

Bus: M6, M15 to South Ferry

Entry fees: Free

Type: History

Museum Shop: No

Restaurant: No

Disabled Access: Yes

Castle Clinton was originally built as a fortress in the early part of the 19th century to protect New York City from attack by the French and the British. No shots were ever fired from this site, however, and over the years the fort served in a variety of other capacities. It first became headquarters for the Third Military District, then changed to a public entertainment center called the Castle Garden. It also functioned as an immigrant landing depot as well as the site of the New York City Aquarium. Today Castle Clinton, named for De Witt Clinton, a former mayor of New York City and later governor of the state, is a national monument that serves as a visitors' center for the national parks in Manhattan. It is located in the center of Battery Park at the southern tip of Manhattan.

The interior of the original building has been renovated and serves as a small museum. Its ongoing exhibitions accentuate the history of Castle Clinton and its numerous transitions over time.

Tickets for the ferry to Ellis Island and Statue of Liberty can be purchased in the courtyard.

China Institute Gallery (Manhattan, Upper East Side)

125 East 65th Street
New York, New York 10021
(212) 744-8181

Open: Daily. Monday–Saturday 10–5; Tuesday 10–8; Sunday 1–5. Call ahead to get current exhibition information.

Entry fees: Yes. Suggested donation

Type: Chinese art and culture

Subway: 6 to 68th Street; N, R to 59th Street

Bus: M1, M2, M3, M4, M101, M102, M103

Museum Shop: Yes

Restaurant: No

Disabled Access: No

The China Institute is recognized internationally for its special exhibitions of Chinese art which spans a period of time from the neolithic period to the 20th century. It is also a part of the China Institute in America, a nonprofit, apolitical organization that promotes understanding between American and Chinese people.

City Hall Governor's Room (Lower Manhattan)

City Hall Park
(Broadway and Park Row)
New York, New York 10007
(212) 788-3071

Open: Monday–Friday 10–12, 1–3:30

Closed: Saturday, Sunday

Entry fees: Free

Type: History

Subway: 2, 3, 4, 5, 6, A, E, C, N, R

Bus: M1, M6, M15, M101, M102

Museum Shop: No. City Books on Chambers Street at north end of park has City Hall-related items, books, cards, posters.

Restaurant: No

Disabled Acess: Yes

The Governor's Room at City Hall is a spacious and ornate reception room where kings, queens, heads of state, celebrities, and heroes have been honored. It's called the Governor's Room because when City Hall was completed in 1812, the room was designated for use by New York's governor whenever he visited the city. It was later expanded to include two smaller side rooms to accommodate City Hall's growing art collection, and today it functions as a museum.

Many special moments have occurred on this site over the years. It was at City Hall in April 1865 that Abraham Lincoln's body lay in state on the landing of the central staircase near the Governor's Room as more than 100,000 mourners paid their respects. And it's also here that many of the ticker-tape parades honoring celebrities and heroes end their march up Broadway.

Highlights: On display in the central room are original Federal-style furnishings and portraits of great Americans, famous city officials, and military heroes. The writing table was used by George Washington at Federal Hall. Over the fireplaces at each end of the room are portraits by John Trumbull of George Washington and George Clinton, New York's first governor. Changing exhibitions feature topics about the history of City Hall.

* The Cloisters (Manhattan, Washington Heights, Upper West Side)

Fort Tryon Park
New York, New York 10040
(212) 923-2700
Open: Tuesday–Sunday 9:30–4:45 (November–February);
Tuesday–Sunday 9:30–5:15 (March–October)
Closed: Monday
Entry fees: Yes
Type: Medieval Art
Subway: 8th Avenue A train to 190th Street. Exit station by elevator, then follow Margaret Corbin Drive or take M4 bus one stop to museum.
Bus: M4 (Fort Tryon-Cloisters to last stop)
Museum Shop: Yes

Restaurant: No
Disabled Access: Limited at entry. Check with security person upon arrival or call in advance.

Step into The Cloisters and you'll feel as though you've taken a 700-year journey back in time. This beautiful museum, an extension of The Metropolitan Museum of Art, is situated in Fort Tryon Park on a spectacular hilltop site at the northern tip of Manhattan Island.

The building is a unique blend of the old and the new. It consists of clusters of rooms, chapels, and even a chapter house, built around four (and a portion of a fifth) medieval cloisters reconstructed in the 1930s by architect Charles Collens Jr. The result is the creation of a serene environment that suggests life in the Middle Ages.

Among numerous treasures you'll find monumental figural sculptures, precious ivories, elaborately illuminated medieval manuscripts, exquisite stained-glass windows, gold and silver reliquaries, jewelry, and, of course, the world famous *Unicorn Tapestries*. Before you begin your visit you should ask for a floor plan of the Museum at the information desk.

Highlights on the main level include the following:
The Campin Room: an intimate domestic 15th-century interior with furnishings and decorative objects that closely duplicate the scene in Robert Campin's *Annunciation Triptych* (also called the Merode Altarpiece) which hangs in the room.
The Unicorn Tapestries Room: *The Unicorn in Captivity.* Include a visit to the 12th-century **Saint-Michael-de-Cuxa Cloister**, the **Saint-Guilhem-Le Desert Cloister**, and **The Gothic Chapel.**

Campin, *Altarpiece of the Annunciation*

The Unicorn in Captivity

The Treasury, situated on the lower level, contains many religious and secular items. Look for **The Cloisters Cross,** The Virgin and Child Reliquary, the Ape Beaker, and *Les Belles Heures*, a lavishly illustrated 15th-century prayer book by the Limbourg Brothers.

Looking back: The medieval architectural materials incorporated into The Cloisters came through the efforts of the American sculptor, George Grey Barnard, who lived in France during the early part of this century. During his travels around the French coutryside he collected columns, capitals, and other architectural fragments from the abandoned monasteries. These were then shipped to the United States and put on public display in New York City in a special building not far from The Cloisters' present location. When the collection went up for sale, it caught the attention of John D. Rockefeller, Jr. He donated funds to The Metropolitan Museum of Art for their purchase and added numerous medieval sculptures from his own collection to the continuing exhibition. Later, Rockefeller gave the land that became Fort Tryon Park to the city of New York with the proviso that its hilltop site be reserved for the construction of a museum of medieval art. This ultimately became The Cloisters, which opened in 1938.

The Cloisters, interior view

* Cooper-Hewitt National Design Museum/ Smithsonian, National Institute of Design (Manhattan, Upper East Side)

2 East 91st Street at Fifth Avenue
New York, New York 10128
(212) 860-6868

Open: Tuesday 10–9;
Wednesday–Saturday 10-5; Sunday
12–5

Closed: Monday

Entry fees: Yes

Type: Art. Design and decorative arts

Subway: Lexington Avenue 4, 5,
and 6 to 86th Street Station

Bus: M1, M2, M3, M4

Museum Shop: Yes

Restaurant: No

Disabled Access:
Call (212) 860-6868

The Cooper-Hewitt National Design Museum is the only museum in the United States dedicated to all aspects of historical and contemporary design. The collection is both large and distinguished, with a quarter of a million objects that span 3,000 years of design including textiles, drawings and prints, jewelry, wall coverings, woodwork, ceramics, glass, furniture, and countless other categories of ornament.

The collection was started in the latter part of the 1800s by Amelia, Eleanor, and Sarah Hewitt, the three granddaughters of Peter Cooper, a wealthy inventor and philanthropist. They shared a passion for gathering objects and materials that were well-crafted. With their unerring eye for excellent design, high quality materials, and workmanship, the women amassed one of the largest collections anywhere of textiles, wallcoverings, jewelry, and countless other objects of innovative design.

In 1897, using their vast resources as a core for research and education, the sisters established the Cooper Union Museum for the Arts and Decoration located in Lower Manhattan on the fourth floor of the Cooper Union for the Advancement of Science and Art, founded in 1859 by their grandfather, Peter Cooper. For almost 100 years the museum thrived and the collections grew.

In 1967 the collections were transferred to the care of the Smithsonian Institution. The Carnegie Corporation donated the 64-room Andrew Carnegie Mansion, complete with terrace and garden, to the Smithsonian Institution to house the collection, and in 1976 the Museum opened under its new name, Cooper-Hewitt National Design Museum.

Highlights: Imaginatively presented exhibitions demonstrate how objects of endless variety are designed—be they mass-produced or individually crafted—with an emphasis on concepts, materials, process, and how these objects of design affect our daily lives. The mansion is itself a showcase, and some of the high points include the glassed-in

Conservatory, filled with ferns and flowers; this is one of the prettiest spots in New York City. Don't miss the **Garden Room** with Tiffany glass panels, the Scottish-oak paneled **Great Hall,** and the **Terrace and Gardens,** a secluded and wonderful urban flowered space open to all. Be sure to check out the museum store which features a variety of well-designed gift items including toys, games, cards, household items, and decorative objects.

Ellis Island Immigration Museum (New York Harbor)

See pages 36–43 for detailed information.

* Federal Hall National Monument (Lower Manhattan)

26 Wall Street at Nassau Street
New York, New York 10005
(212) 825-6888

Open: Daily 9–5

Closed: Major holidays except Washington's Birthday and July 4th

Entry fees: Free

Type: American History

Subway: 2, 3, 4, 5, J, M, R, N

Bus: M1, M6, M15

Entry fees: Free

Museum Shop: Yes

Restaurant: No

Disabled Access: Yes; entry at 15 Pine Street

On this site, at what was the original City Hall building, some of the most significant events in early American history took place: the first fight for freedom of the press, the rally against taxation, and the decision to organize the convention which created our present form of government. It is also where Congress developed our Bill of Rights, established the U.S. Treasury, the Supreme Court, and the departments of State and War.

In 1788, the Confederated Congress named New York City the capital of the United States, and it was here that George Washington gave his first inaugural address on the balcony of the original City Hall building on April 30, 1789.

The present building, Greek Revival in its design, was completed in 1842 and was used as the U.S. Customs House. Later it became the U.S. Subtreasury building. Today it is an important museum that devotes itself, through exhibits and displays, to the events that shaped our government in its earliest days. **Highlights:** In the **Rotunda** there are exhibits on the architecture of Federal Hall and the two buildings that preceded it. In the **George Washington Room** see the plain brown suit worn by Washington on Inauguration Day; the Bible used at the inauguration; a diorama of the inauguration parade from Washington's home on Cherry Street to Federal Hall. **East Gallery:** IBM's *A Promise of Permanency* exhibit on the development and the meaning of our Constitution. **West Gallery:** Video presentation entitled *Journey to Federal Hall* that describes historical events that took place on this site. **Second Floor:** rotating exhibits and educational displays presented by the National Park Service and other organizations on American politics, history, architecture.

* Forbes Magazine Galleries (Manhattan, Murray Hill)

62 Fifth Avenue at 12th Street
New York, New York 10011
(212) 206-5548

Open: Tuesday, Wednesday, Friday, Saturday 10–4; Thursdays reserved for group tours. Entry on first-come, first-served basis. Children must be with an adult; four children maximum per adult.

Closed: Sunday, Monday, legal holidays

Entry fees: Free

Type: Art, history

Subway: Westside 1, 2, 3; East Side 4, 5, 6; N, R, Q, L

Bus: M2, M3, M5, M6, M14

Museum Shop: No

Restaurant: No

Disabled Access: Yes

The Forbes Magazine collection, assembled by Malcolm Forbes and his sons, showcases a fascinating if eclectic mix of treasures that range from miniature boats to one of the world's preeminent collections of Fabergé eggs, surpassed only by that of Britain's Queen Elizabeth II. All of this is displayed in innovatively designed galleries that incorporate theme music appropriate to each collection.

Highlights: *Ships Ahoy* includes 500 antique toy boats, 5 models of *Highlanders* yachts owned by Forbes, and gold ground-glass panels and fittings from the Grand Salon of the *Normandie*. *On Parade* features the famous collection of 12,000 miniature toy soldiers, set up as reenact-

ments of actual battles. *Monopoly* features several versions of Monopoly as the game evolved to its present form. The *Presidential Papers* galleries have selections from the magazine's 3,000 American historical documents and memorabilia including papers that reveal intimate glimpses into the lives, personalities, and works of American presidents. Three miniature rooms designed by Eugene Kupjack include Washington's headquarters for the battle of Yorktown, Virginia, John Adams' kitchen law office in Braintree, Massachusetts, and Jefferson's bedroom and study at Monticello, Virginia.

The most stunning part of the collection is featured in the **Fabergé Gallery** where 12 of the fabled Fabergé Easter eggs, designed especially for the last two czars of Russia, are displayed. Other lavish decorative objects are here as well, and don't overlook the miniature room, an exact copy of Czarina Alexandra's Sitting Room in the Alexandrovsky Palace, also designed by Eugene Kupjack.

Forbes Magazine Galleries is one of the oldest corporate collections in America and one of the few open to the public free of charge.

Fraunces Tavern Museum (Lower Manhattan, Financial District)

54 Pearl Street (Corner of Pearl and Broad Streets)
New York, New York 10004
(212) 425-1778

Open: Monday–Friday 10–4:45; Saturday 12–4; some holidays, some evenings (call first for information)

Closed: Sunday, major holidays except Washington's Birthday and July 4th

Entry fees: Yes

Type: History, Early American

Subway: 1, 9 to South Ferry; 2, 3 to Wall Street; 4, 5 to Bowling Green; N, R to Whitehall

Bus: M1, M6, M15 to South Ferry

Museum Shop: Yes

Restaurant: No (Fraunces Tavern, the restaurant located on the first floor, is a completely separate enterprise which is not run by the museum.)

Disabled Access: No

The Fraunces Tavern Museum is one of the oldest and best-known landmarks in New York City, and is listed in the National Register of Historic Places. It occupies the second and third floors of this building.

The tavern was originally a town home built for Stephen DeLancey in 1719. Samuel Fraunces subsequently bought the residence and converted it to a tavern. It quickly grew in popularity and became a favorite gathering place for merchants and patriots including George Washington. It was here that Washington gave his farewell address to the officers of the Continental Army. He later used the tavern for offices of the new government's departments of War, Foreign Affairs, and Treasury.

Highlights: The Long Room, site of Washington's farewell to his officers, now restored to its original appearance, and the Clinton Room, a duplication of an early 19th-century dining room. There are also changing exhibitions on different topics of early American history and culture.

✳ The Frick Collection (Manhattan, Upper East Side)

1 East 70th Street and Fifth Avenue
New York, New York 10021
(212) 288-0700

Open: Tuesday–Saturday 10–6; Sunday 1–6

Closed: Monday, major holidays

Entry fees: Yes. Children under 16 must be with an adult. Children under 10 not admitted.

Type: Art

Subway: 6

Bus: M1, M2, M3, M4, M29, M30

Museum Shop: Yes

Restaurant: No

Disabled Access: Yes. Wheelchair available. Call first.

The Frick Collection epitomizes the perfect art museum: it's not too large, the setting is utterly charming, and the collections, especially the paintings, are superb. Artists such as Rembrandt, Gainsborough, Vermeer, and Velázquez are among the superstars, and at every turn there's a wide range of decorative objects to admire: fine 18th-century French furniture, bronzes, oriental rugs, Limoges enamels, and much more, all in superb condition.

Sometime during your tour, be sure to visit the barrel-vaulted glass-topped Garden Court with its fountain and reflecting pool. Visitors find this a serene place to relax. Also well worth seeing is a 20-minute audio-visual, *The Frick Collection, an Introduction*, shown hourly in the Music Room from 10:30 to 4:30, except on Sundays when concerts are scheduled. **Highlights:** Because everything here is so special, choices are difficult to make. The following are some of the author's favorites: in the **West Vestibule:** *The Four Seasons* by Francois Boucher; **South Hall:** *Officer and the Laughing Girl* by Vermeer (one of the Frick Collection's great prizes); also in the same room, *Mother and Children* by Pierre-Auguste Renoir. **The Fragonard Room:** Fragonard's famous Rococo masterpiece series, *The Progress of Love*. In the **Living Hall** look for the compelling portrait of *Sir Thomas More* by Hans Holbein the Younger, and *St. Francis in the Desert* by Bellini. The **West Gallery,** the largest of all the galleries, has numerous masterpieces including Bronzino's *Lodovico Capponi, The White Horse* by Constable, Rembrandt's *Self Portrait,* and *King Philip IV of Spain* by Velázquez.

Fragonard, *Love Letters*

Rembrandt, *Self Portrait*

General Grant's Tomb (Manhattan, Upper West Side)

Riverside Drive at 122nd Street
New York, New York
(212) 666-1640

Open: Daily 9–5

Closed: Christmas

Entry fees: Voluntary donation

Type: History

Subway: 1 to 116th Street

Bus: 5th Avenue to 116th Street or 125th and Broadway, or the 125th Street crosstown bus 5 goes directly to Grant's Tomb

Museum Shop: Yes

Restaurant: No

Disabled Access: No. There are many steps.

The unassuming Ulysses S. Grant was a great hero of the American Civil War, president of the United States and world statesman and traveler. His funeral procession, August 8, 1885, was one of the most splendid ever to be held for an American, with a seven-mile-long procession made up of more than 60,000 people, the whole of Congress, the Supreme Court justices, and President Grover Cleveland and his cabinet.

Grant's Tomb, the largest mausoleum in America, stands on a bluff overlooking the Hudson River. Architect John Duncan's design is a composite of some of the most famous monuments to individuals the world over, among them the emperor Hadrian in Rome, King Mausolus at Halicarnassus (now Turkey), and Emperor Napoleon in Paris. **Highlights** include a photo display of significant moments in Grant's life, portraits, and documents. Three large murals show General Grant engaged

in the Civil War battles of Vicksburg, Chattanooga and Appomattox.

* The Solomon R. Guggenheim Museum (Manhattan, Upper East Side)

1071 Fifth Avenue (at 88th Street)
New York, New York 10128
(212) 423-3500
(212) 360-3513
(exhibition information)

Open: Sunday–Wednesday 10–6; Friday–Saturday, 10–8

Closed: Thursday and Christmas

Entry fees: Yes

Type: Art

Subway: 4, 5, or 6 train on Lexington Avenue line to 86th Street

Bus: M1, M2, M3, M4

Museum Shop: Yes

Restaurant: Yes

Disabled Access: Yes

The first thing you notice inside the Guggenheim Museum is a fantastic spiral ramp that coils upward to a spectacular skylight. Paintings and sculpture are displayed in cubicles along its winding path, making this one of the most unique places in the world to experience art in an enclosed setting. So spectacular is this Frank Lloyd Wright-designed structure, the city of New York has recently designated it a landmark, an honor normally bestowed on much older buildings.

The Guggenheim Museum has recently undergone an extensive expansion program to handle its large collection. It now incorporates handsome new galleries for showing large-scale art, and a new sculpture terrace with a great view of Central Park.

Its impressive permanent holdings include the world's largest collection of paintings by Kandinsky, a sizeable number of works by Paul Klee and just about everyone else who has been important in the art of the Western world in this century. Many exciting special exhibitions complement Solomon Guggenheim's collection of 20th-century art. Theme shows explore ideas, methods, historical and political subjects in art, while others concentrate solely on well-known artists such as Francis Bacon, Louise Nevelson, David Smith, Mark Rothko, and Morris Louis.

The Justin K. Thannhauser collection, which comprises representational works by the Impressionist and Post-Impressionist schools and the School of Paris, is on permanent display on the second, third, and fourth levels. **Highlights** from this collection include: *Woman with a Parrot,* by Pierre-Auguste Renoir; *In the Vanilla Grove,* by Paul Gauguin; Toulouse Lautrec's *Au Salon; Farm Women at Work,* by Georges Seurat; Edgar Degas' *Dancers in Green and Yellow;* and three outstanding works by Pablo Picasso: **Le Moulin de la Galette; Woman Ironing;** and **Woman With Yellow Hair.**

Picasso, *Woman Ironing*

Degas, *Dancers in Green and Yellow*

Guggenheim Museum SoHo (Manhattan, SoHo)

575 Broadway at Prince Street
New York, New York 10012
(212) 423-3500

Open: Sunday, Wednesday–Friday 11–6; Saturday 11–8

Closed: Monday–Tuesday

Entry fees: Yes. Children under 12 free when accompanied by an adult

Type: Art

Subway: 6 train on Lexington Avenue line to Spring Street Station

Bus: M1 Fifth Avenue to Broadway and Prince Street; or M10 and M6

Museum Shop: Yes

Restaurant: No

Disabled Access: Yes

Special exhibitions and selections from the permanent collection are featured in this spacious newly renovated 19th-century landmark building ornamented with wrought iron.

Hispanic Society of America (Manhattan, Washington Heights)

613 West 155th Street
Audubon Terrace, Broadway
at 155th Street
New York, New York 10032
(212) 926-2234

Open: Tuesday–Saturday 10–4:30; Sunday 1–4. Library reading room open Tuesday–Friday 1–4:15

Closed: Monday, major holidays

Entry fees: Free

Type: Art and history of Spain and Portugal

Subway: 1, B, M

Bus: M4, M5, M100, M101

Shop: Yes

Restaurant: No

Disabled Access: No, call ahead

Over this century the Hispanic Society of America has become an important research center for Spanish and Portuguese history, art, and literature. The facility is a combination museum and library with over 200,000 books, maps, and literary works. The galleries showcase works of art from prehistory to the present.

Highlights: Among its treasures you'll find paintings by Goya, Velázquez, El Greco, and Ribera, prints, sculpture, tiles, tombs, decorative arts, and numerous other important objects all from the Iberian Peninsula. Its high-ceilinged main gallery is quite impressive.

Historic Richmond Town/Staten Island Historical Society

441 Clark Avenue
Staten Island, New York 10306
(718) 351-1611

Open: Wednesday–Sunday 1–5. Hours can vary seasonally. Call ahead.

Closed: Monday, Tuesday, Thanksgiving, Christmas, New Year's Day, Easter Sunday

Entry fees: Yes

Type: Historic site. Restoration of Staten Island's original county seat

Transportation: Take the Staten Island Ferry from Battery Park, then bus S74.

Museum Shop: Yes

Restaurant: Yes

Disabled Access: Yes. You should call ahead.

Take a step back in time and visit the tiny settlement of Richmond Town, a 200-year-old settlement once known as "Cocclestown," so named for the oysters and clams once found there. It has been restored to represent daily life in Staten Island as it would

have been experienced from the 17th to the early 20th centuries.

The 100-acre site is dotted with numerous buildings in a variety of architectural styles, each containing antique furnishings and toys, costumes, and vehicles. Visitors can wander through shops, a general store, a school, and farmhouses, and watch as the Richmond Town staff, dressed in authentic early-American costumes, reenact a variety of trades (seasonally). The center offers a variety of programs for children and adults year-round including crafts demonstrations, lectures, fairs, concerts, and art exhibitions.

International Center of Photography (Manhattan, Upper East Side)

1130 Fifth Avenue
at East 94th Street
(Midtown extension located at 1133 Avenue of the Americas at 43rd Street)
New York, New York 10128
(212) 860-1777

Open: Tuesday 11–8; Wednesday–Sunday 11–6

Closed: Monday

Entry fees: Yes. Voluntary contribution. Free Tuesday 6–8

Type: Art

Bus: M1, M2, M3, M4, Crosstown M19

Museum Shop: Yes

Restaurant: No

Disabled Access: Yes, with assistance

From commercial photography to still-life composition, from photojournalism to darkroom technique and all the stops (no pun) in between, this is the place to visit if you enjoy any aspect of the photographic medium.

The special exhibitions are so well done that they often travel to museums and universities around the United States and abroad, and the permanent collection of master photographs is one of the most comprehensive in the country.

The center has featured the works of more than 2,500 photographers since its opening in 1974, including such luminaries as Dorothea Lange, Henri Cartier Bresson, Alfred Eisenstadt, Man Ray, and David Hockney. Aside from its excellent ongoing exhibitions, special programs abound in this exciting center. You can avail yourself of workshops and lectures, use its acclaimed archives and resource library, and even earn a master's degree in photography.

Isamu Noguchi Museum and Gardens (Long Island City)

32-37 Vernon Park Boulevard (off of Vernon Boulevard at 33rd Road) Long Island City, New York 11106 (718) 204-7088

Open: Wednesday, Thursday, Friday 10–5; Saturday–Sunday 11–6 (April through November)

Closed: December through March

Entry fees: Yes. Suggested donation

Type: Art

Subway: N train to Broadway stop in Queens. You will be at the corner of Broadway and 31st Street. Walk down Broadway towards the Manhattan skyline (towards the East River) until Broadway ends at Vernon Boulevard. Turn left on Vernon and go two blocks. The museum is on the left side of the street at the corner of Vernon Boulevard and 33rd Road. The entrance is on 33rd Road. Allow about 15 minutes for walk from subway.

Bus: Q104; or via weekend shuttle bus from Manhattan on Saturdays and Sundays. Leaves from the Asia Society, Park Avenue at 70th Street, hourly from 11:30 A.M.

Museum Shop: Yes

Restaurant: No

Disabled Access: Limited. Call ahead.

This important museum dedicates itself to exhibiting the works of Isamu Noguchi, one of the most gifted and prolific Japanese-American artists of the 20th century. The permanent collection includes 300 of his works in stone, metal, clay, and wood, and his famous "Akari" light sculptures. Also on view are models of sets Noguchi designed for Martha Graham's dance productions and countless plans for gardens, public plazas, and playgrounds he designed and installed in cities around the world. Guided tours are available by appointment.

Jacques Marchais Museum of Tibetan Art (Staten Island)

338 Lighthouse Avenue Staten Island, New York 10306 (718) 987-3500

Open: Wednesday–Sunday 1–5, April through November. Open by appointment only from mid-November through March. Call (718) 987-3500 for information.

Closed: Monday, Tuesday

Entry fees: Yes

Type: Art, Tibetan and Buddhist

Transportation: Take the Staten Island Ferry from Battery Park, then bus S74 to Lighthouse Avenue. Walk uphill to the museum.

Museum Shop: Yes

Restaurant: No

Disabled Access: No

At the Jacques Marchais Museum you'll find a small Tibetan temple, set in an idyllic environment, which houses a large collection of Tibetan and Buddhist art. The museum was established by Jacqueline Klauber, whose professional name was Jacques Marchais. In 1945 she established this unique center to showcase her private collection to promote research and interest in Tibetan and Asian cultures. A catalogue of the collections is available and a guide is present to answer questions.

Highlights include the terraced gardens; bronze statuettes including representations of such deities as the eleven-headed Avalokiteshvara and Hayagriva; masks, cloisonné, jewelry, and numerous ethnographic objects.

Japan Society (Midtown Manhattan, East Side)

333 East 47th Street
(between 1st and 2nd Avenues)
New York, New York 10017
(212) 832-1155

Subway: 6, 8th Avenue E, or 6th Avenue F

Bus: M15, M27, M50, M101, or M102

Open: Tuesday–Sunday 11–5 when there is an exhibit. Call ahead.

Closed: Monday, legal holidays

Entry fees: Voluntary contribution

Type: Japanese arts and culture

Shop: Yes; bookstall only

Restaurant: No

Disabled Access: Yes

The Japan Society is an organization that devotes its energies toward the understanding of Japanese culture past and present. Lectures and cultural programs focus on history, politics, literature, commerce, and the arts. The Society's excellent special art exhibitions feature the best in traditional and contemporary paintings, sculpture, prints, architectural design, decorative arts, and much more. The gallery hosts as many as three exhibitions per year, each lasting about two months. Call ahead for current exhibition information.

The Jewish Museum (Manhattan, Upper East Side)

1109 Fifth Avenue at 92nd Street
New York, New York 10128
(212) 423-3200

Open: Sunday, Monday, Wednesday, Thursday 11–5:45; Tuesday 11–8

Closed: Friday, Saturday, major legal and Jewish holidays

Entry fees: Yes. Free Tuesday 5–8

Type: Art, history

Subway: 1, 2, 3, 9, B, C

Bus: M10, M79

Museum Shop: Yes

Restaurant : Yes; open during museum hours and Friday 11–3

Disabled Access: Ramp on 92nd Street

This important museum is located in the handsome and newly renovated Warburg Mansion, a French Chateau Gothic-style building originally constructed in 1908. Ongoing exhibitions showcase the works of Israeli artists and Jewish artists from other countries plus theme shows that reflect the culture and identity of the Jewish community the world over.

Highlights: Don't miss *Cultures and Continuity: The Jewish Journey,* a permanent exhibition that consists of a re-creation of an ancient synagogue. Also worth seeing are the following: ceremonial art, Holocaust sculpture, paintings, a video on contemporary Judaism, and a film on Jewish ritual.

Lower East Side Tenement Museum (Manhattan, Lower East Side)

90 Orchard Street
(near Broome Street)
New York, New York 10002
(212) 431-0233

Open: Tuesday–Sunday 11–5

Closed: Monday, major holidays

Entry fees: Yes. Building tour and walking tours by arrangement. Call ahead for schedule.

Type: History. Immigrant life in an urban neighborhood.

Subway: B, D, Q to Grand Street; E to Delancey. J, M, Z to Essex Street

Bus: M15

Museum Shop: Yes

Restaurant: No

Disabled Access: No

This is one of New York City's most innovative history museums. Here you can learn about, see, and even feel the urban immigrant experience. Two apartments are preserved in such a way that visitors gain a sense of the extremely crowded conditions endured by a German-Jewish family of the 1870s and a Sicilian family of the 1930s. **Highlights:** Visit Gallery 90 which houses "The Urban Log Cabin," a 6-foot-high scale model of the Museum's 1863 tenement building at 97 Orchard Street. Depression-era photos by Arnold Eagle are on display, as are changing exhibitions that depict the life of immigrant families in New York City over the past 150 years. *South of Delancey* is a 30-minute video featuring interviews with former residents of 97 Orchard Street and today's immigrant residents of the Lower East Side. The *Urban Pioneers* slide show recounts the story of 97 Orchard Street in the context of the Lower East Side.

On weekends you can take guided walking tours. "The Streets Where We Lived" walk demonstrates the ethnic mix of the neighborhood, and "Heritage Walking Tours" explores immigrant communities (tickets required).

The Metropolitan Museum of Art (Manhattan, Upper East Side)

See pages 44–65 for detailed information.

El Museo del Barrio (Manhattan, East Harlem, Upper East Side)

1230 Fifth Avenue (between 104th and 105th Streets)
New York, New York 10029-4496
(212) 831-7272

Open: Wednesday–Sunday 11–5; Thursday 11–7 between May and September

Closed: Monday, Tuesday, major holidays

Entry fees: Yes. Suggested donation

Type: Arts of Puerto Rico and Latin America of contemporary scope

Subway: 6 to 103rd Street Station then walk towards 5th Avenue and 104th Street

Bus: M1, M3, M4 on Madison or 5th Avenues to 104th Street

Museum Shop: Yes

Restaurant: No

Disabled Access: Yes

Since its beginning in 1969, El Museo del Barrio has become one of the foremost cultural institutions representing the full scope and richness of Latin American communities in the City of New York and throughout the country.

The permanent collection has over 8,000 objects spanning 800 years, from the pre-Columbian Arawak civilization in the Caribbean to contemporary art. The collection includes paintings, sculpture, works on paper, photographs, and pre-Columbian artifacts and traditional arts of all kinds including masks and *santos de palo*. Special exhibitions are presented regularly as well as tours and museum talks. The Latin American film and video festival, music, theater, and dance performances will resume in its 640-seat theatre, following its renovation scheduled for completion in 1997. Call ahead for information on current exhibitions and special programs.

Museum for African Art (Manhattan, SoHo)

593 Broadway (between Houston and Prince Streets)
New York, New York 10012
(212) 966-1313

Open: Tuesday–Friday 10:30–5:30; Saturday–Sunday 12–6

Closed: Monday, major holidays

Entry fees: Yes

Type: Art

Subway: 6 (Lexington Avenue line) to Spring or Bleecker Street; N or R (Broadway lines) to Prince Street; B, D, Q, or F to Broadway and Lafayette.

Bus: 6 to the museum entrance; 1, 5 or 21 to Houston Street or Broadway

Museum Shop: Yes

Restaurant: No

Disabled Access: Yes

Having moved from its uptown Manhattan location in 1992, the Museum for African Art is now part of "SoHo Museum Row" along with the Guggenheim Musem SoHo and

the New Museum of Contemporary Art. It is internationally recognized for its excellent and challenging exhibitions on traditional and contemporary African art and culture, and also as a major publisher of books on African art. Examples of recent exhibitions are *Animals in African Art: From the Familiar to the Marvelous*, which explored the relationships between man and animals, and *Exhibition-ism: Museums and African Art*, which examined methodologies for displaying African art.

Workshops, public lectures, scholarly publications, storytelling, and other creative activities for children and parents are offered year-round.

Museum of American Folk Art, Eva and Morris Feld Gallery (Manhattan, Upper West Side)

Columbus Avenue between 65th and 66th Streets
New York, New York 10023-6214
(212) 595-9533

Open: Tuesday–Sunday 11:30–7:30

Closed: Monday, holidays

Entry fees: Free. Voluntary donation appreciated

Type: American folk art

Subway: 1, 9, A, B, C, D

Bus: M5, M7, M10, M30, M66, M104

Museum Shop: Yes

Restaurant: No

Disabled Access: Yes

This lively museum is the country's leading center of American folk art. Founded by a group of scholars in 1961, the Museum is dedicated to preserving the rich folk heritage of the United States through exhibitions, educational programs, special events, and publications of the highest quality. It is impossible to predict what will be on view because exhibitions rotate throughout the year. However, you can always count on seeing an amazing diversity of handmade objects and artifacts that could include paintings and sculpture, handmade valentines, quilts, antique weather vanes, lace, yarn paintings, toys, furniture, and so on. Both children and adults find this one of the most fascinating small museums to visit in New York City.

* Museum of the City of New York (Manhattan, East Harlem)

1220 Fifth Avenue at 103rd Street
New York, New York 10029-5287
(212) 534-1672

Open: Wednesday–Saturday 10–5;
Sunday 1–5

Closed: Monday and Tuesday (except to preregistered school groups) and legal holidays

Entry fees: Suggested contribution

Type: Historical, decorative arts, New York City memorabilia

Subway: 6 (Lexington Avenue line) to 103rd Street then 3 blocks west

Bus: M1, M3, M4 on Madison or 5th Avenues

Museum Shop: Yes

Restaurant: No

Disabled Access: Yes. Use side entrance on 104th Street.

The Museum of the City of New York is a wonderful resource for New Yorkers and newcomers alike who want to learn about the history of America's largest and most dynamic city. Changing special exhibitions draw from its collection of 1.5 million objects to present varying views of the city's cultural diversity, architectural achievements, and economic growth. **Highlights:** A distinguished 2,000-work collection of sculpture and paintings, including cityscapes, genre paintings, marine views, and over 500 portraits of prominent New Yorkers; 300,000 photographs documenting New York; a silver collection that is one of the foremost public collections of its kind in the United States; a costume collection with 25,000 articles; and a toy collection that includes 25,000 playthings. Often on view are selections from the American theater memorabilia collection including costumes worn by famous performers in operas, plays, and musicals. Period rooms include a bedroom from the residence of John D. Rockefeller, and there is a wonderful assortment of dollhouses. A great place to browse.

* The Museum of Modern Art (Midtown Manhattan, West Side)

See pages 66–81 for detailed information.

* National Academy Museum and School of the Fine Arts (Manhattan, Upper East Side)

1083 Fifth Avenue at 89th Street
New York, New York 10128
(212) 369-4880

Open: Wednesday–Sunday 12–5;
Friday 12–8

Closed: Monday and Tuesday

Entry fees: Yes

Type: Art

Subway: Lexington Avenue trains 4, 5, or 6 to 86th Street; walk to Fifth Avenue and then north to 89th Street

Bus: M1, M2, M3, M4 to 89th Street

Museum Shop: Yes

Restaurant: No

Disabled Access: Yes

Situated on the Museum Mile in a beautiful turn-of-the-century Fifth Avenue mansion, the National Academy of Design is one of New York City's great hidden treasures. It is an art school of great distinction, an honorary organization of artists, and a museum all rolled into one, with one of the world's foremost collections of 19th- and 20th-century American art. Included in its permanent collection of 8,000 paintings, sculptures, prints, and drawings are works by leading artists and architects such as Mary Cassatt, William Merritt Chase, Richard Diebenkorn, Norman Rockwell, Ben Shahn, I. M. Pei, Robert Rauschenberg, John Singer Sargent, and Frank Lloyd Wright.

The school of fine arts, modeled on the great European art academies, was founded in 1825 by Samuel F. B. Morse, Thomas Cole, and other prominent American artists. As the second oldest and most distinguished art academy in America, it boasts a long list of famous former students including Winslow Homer, Adolph Gottlieb, Lee Krasner, Augustus Saint-Gaudens, Ben Shahn, and William Baziotes.

Highlights: Special exhibitions feature selections from the permanent collection and works by American and European artists. Educational programs for visitors include lectures, concerts, symposia, special tours, and artist's talks.

* National Museum of the American Indian/ Smithsonian Institution George Gustave Heye Center (Lower Manhattan)

1 Bowling Green
New York, New York 10004
(212) 825-6700

Open: Daily 10–5

Closed: Christmas

Entry fees: Free

Type: Arts, crafts, history of the American Indian

Subway: 4, 5 to Bowling Green; 1, 9 to South Ferry, walk four blocks north; N, R to Whitehall Street

Bus: M1, M6, M15 to South Ferry

Museum Shop: Yes

Restaurant: No

Disabled Access: Yes

The Smithsonian Institution's George Gustave Heye Center, located in the Alexander Hamilton Custom House in Lower Manhattan, is one of New York City's newest museums. Its considerable collections span 10,000 years of the history and art of Native American Indian tribes, and its special exhibitions examine the current cultures of native peoples from all over the Western Hemisphere.

Take time to meander through the numerous displays that feature the very best examples of native artifacts including blankets, baskets, tools, pottery, clothing, jewelry, paintings, sculptures, and dolls. In addition there is an excellent resource center located near the main entrance that has computers, discovery boxes, books, and videos for use by visitors who want to learn more about native communities throughout the Western Hemisphere.

The New Museum of Contemporary Art (Manhattan, SoHo)

583 Broadway (between
Prince Street and Houston Street)
New York, New York 10012
(212) 219-1222
(212) 219-1355
(recorded information)

Open: Wednesday, Thursday, Sunday
12–6; Friday–Saturday 12–8

Closed: Monday, Tuesday, legal
holidays

Entry fees: Yes. Children under
12 free

Type: Contemporary Art

Subway: 6, A, C, E, F, and N, R, D,
Q, F

Bus: M1, M5, M6, M21 to Houston
Street

Museum Shop: Yes

Restaurant: No

Disabled Access: Partial; call ahead

If you want to see what and who is
on the forefront of contemporary art,
this is the place to visit. The New
Museum of Contemporary Art presents works in all media made in the
last ten years, primarily by living
artists. Committed to an ongoing
investigation of what art is and the
roles art plays in society, the Museum
provides a public forum for express-
ing diverse points of view through its
exhibitions, publications, and public
programs. Thought-provoking shows
in the recent past have included
internationally known artists such as
Andres Serrano, Vito Acconci, Joan
Brown, Judy Chicago, John Baldessari,
and Dennis Oppenheim.

* The New York Historical Society (Manhattan, Upper West Side)

170 Central Park West
at West 77th Street
New York, New York 10024
(212) 873-3400

Open: Wednesday–Sunday 12–5

Closed: Monday, Tuesday, public
holidays

Entry fees: Yes. Suggested donation

Type: History, emphasis on New York

Subway: B or C train to 81st Street

Bus: M7, M10, M11; Crosstown:
M72, M79

Museum Shop: Yes

Restaurant: Coffee and tea

Disabled Access: Must call ahead

This important center, established in
1804, has vast holdings in American
painting, sculpture, photographs, the
decorative arts, documents, manuscripts, literary works, and more. The
Society draws upon its excellent collections to present imaginative exhibitions that capture the spirit of New
York and how the city has evolved
over the past 200 years. **Highlights:**
Among many excellent possibilities,
make it a point to see the glorious
landscapes by Hudson River School
artists, Tiffany lamps, photographs
and maps of old New York, and John
James Audubon's watercolors for *The
Birds of America.*

* New York Public Library (Midtown Manhattan, West Side)

5th Avenue and 42nd Street
New York, New York 10018-2788
(212) 340-0849
(212) 869-8089
(current exhibition information)

Open: Monday 10–6;
Tuesday–Wednesday 11–7:30;
Thursday–Saturday 10–6

Closed: Sunday, major holidays

Entry fees: Free

Type: Library, research, art and historical exhibits

Subway: 7 to 42nd Street;
D to 42nd Street

Bus: M1, M2, M3, M4 to
42nd Street

Museum Shop: Yes

Restaurant: No

Disabled Access: Yes

This venerable institution, which recently celebrated its 100th year (1895–1995) is considered one of the world's greatest libraries. It operates four research centers (Center for the Humanities; Schomburg Center for Research in Black Culture; The New York Public Library for the Performing Arts; and the Science, Industry, and Business Library) and 82 branch libraries in three boroughs of New York City. Its combined collections are vast, with 18 million books, works of art, rare books and manuscripts, prints, maps, photographs, and more.

You can't help but notice the New York Public Library because it's one of the city's most distinctive landmarks, stretching along two entire city blocks, with its two great Tennessee pink marble lions, Patience and Fortitude, flanking its stairway. Once inside this Beaux Arts masterpiece designed by Carrère and Hastings, visitors can fully appreciate its awesome proportions as they enter the monumental Astor Hall and wander through its various reading rooms, exhibition galleries, and open rotundas.

A look around the building is a must for visitors. **Highlights:** Ongoing special exhibitions of art, rare books, manuscripts, and maps can be seen throughout the library, as well as special theme presentations. On the first floor visit **Gottesman Exhibition Hall** with its white marble walls and oak ceiling. This beautiful space provides a grand setting for major exhibitions that draw from both the Library's collections and those of other institutions. Take a look at the **DeWitt Wallace Periodicals Room,** also elaborately adorned with marble and a ceiling of molded plaster (treated to resemble wood) with murals of buildings of the major New York publishers by artist Richard Haas. Visit the beautiful **Celeste Bartos Forum,** located on the ground level opposite the 42nd Street entrance, with its 30-foot-high glass saucer dome and yellow Siena marble walls. On the third floor go into the **Edna Barnes Solomon Room** which has the Library's permanent paintings collection as well as changing exhibitions; take note of the **McGraw Rotunda,** festooned with murals by Edward Laning representing the history of the printed word; the **Main Reading Room** is a must, if only to admire its size (297 feet long by 78 feet wide) and its spectacularly ornate ceiling; also visit the **Catalog Room,** with large windows and information desk and the **Berg Collection Exhibition Room** where excellent literary exhibitions are held.

To get the very best from this building, you can take a one-hour tour to learn fascinating facts about the art and architecture. Tours depart from the Information Desk in Astor Hall at 11 A.M. and 2 P.M.

Nicholas Roerich Museum (Manhattan, Upper West Side)

319 West 107th Street
at Riverside Drive
New York, New York 10025-2799
(212) 864-7752

Open: Tuesday–Sunday 2–5

Closed: Monday, legal holidays

Entry fees: Voluntary contribution

Type: Art

Subway: 1, 9

Bus: M5, M104

Museum Shop: Yes

Restaurant: No

Disabled Access: Call ahead

Nicholas Roerich, Russian scholar, artist, philosopher, educator and humanitarian, was devoted to the ideals of achieving world harmony through art and culture and worked tirelessly toward that end. The result of his dedication led to the establishment of this appealing museum, situated in an elegant Manhattan townhouse, where three floors are given over to a display of Roerich's colorful paintings. Especially notable are the Himalayan landscapes executed during the years Roerich lived in India. The museum presents special exhibitions of works by emerging and established artists and a variety of other programs including chamber music, recitals, and art lectures.

* Pierpont Morgan Library (Manhattan, Murray Hill, East Side)

29 East 36th Street
and Madison Avenue
New York, New York 10016-3490
(212) 685-0008
(212) 285-0610
(recorded information)

Open: Tuesday–Friday 10:30–5; Saturday 10:30–6; Sunday 12–6

Closed: Monday, major holidays

Entry fees: Suggested contribution

Type: Library/emphasis on art, rare books, and manuscripts

Subway: 6

Bus: M1, M2, M3, M4, M5, M34

Museum Shop: Yes

Restaurant: Yes, the Morgan Court Café. Tuesday–Friday 11–4; Saturday 11–5; Sunday 12–5

Disabled Access: Yes. Help is available to negotiate some low steps into the original building. Full access inside.

J. P. Morgan, a leading financier at the turn of the century, was one of the world's great collectors with a special passion for rare books and manuscripts. Morgan hired Charles McKim to design an elegant and intimate Renaissance-style palazzo adjacent to his home to hold his personal library. The structure was built between 1902 and 1906, and although there have been several additions to the site, including a spectacular glass atrium that connects the main building to a new gift shop and restaurant, the building maintains its original beauty and charm. Highly acclaimed special exhibitions are offered year-round.

Highlights: In the **West Room,** Morgan's personal study, note the antique wooden ceiling from Florence, incorporated into the room by architect Charles McKim; stained glass window panels of the 15th and 16th centuries; the mantelpiece by Florentine sculptor Desidirio da Settignano (c. 1430–1464); two portraits of J. P. Morgan by Frank Holl and Frank O. Salisbury; and Morgan's desk.

The *pièce de résistance* is the East Room, filled to the rafters (literally) with rare books, manuscripts, original musical scores, and more. Three tiers of bronze bookcases line the walls on all sides, with shelves of glass to protect the books from splinters. Concealed in corners are stairways hidden behind bookcases that allow access to the upper tiers (public not allowed). Always on display is a Gutenberg Bible; a life mask of George Washington done in 1785 by Jean Antoine Houdon; a 35-page summary of Einstein's theory of relativity, in his own hand; letters from Balzac, Keats, and Jane Austen; a 9th-century jeweled book cover of the Lindau Gospels; love letters from Napoleon to Josephine, and many more rare and fascinating works.

✴ **Queens Museum of Art (Queens)**

New York City Building
Flushing Meadows-Corona Park
Flushing, New York 11368
(718) 592-9700

Open: Wednesday–Friday 10–5; Saturday–Sunday 12–5

Closed: Monday; Tuesday, open to groups by appointment; public holidays

Entry fees: Yes. Children under 5 free

Type: Art

Subway: 7 Flushing line, exit Willets Point/Shea Stadium. Follow signs to the museum.

Bus: Q48 to Roosevelt Avenue and 111th Street; Q58 to Corona Avenue and 51st Avenue; Q23

Museum Shop: Yes

Restaurant: No

Disabled Access: Yes

One of the great claims to fame of this newly renovated art museum is "The Panorama of the City of New York," the world's largest architectural scale model of a metropolitan area, which has 895,00 individual buildings. This major tourist attraction, which has been on-site since the 1964 New York World's Fair, was recently renovated and now boasts 60,000 changes and additions.

Programs galore emanate from here as well, including "The Looking Series," a slide, film, and lecture series about the materials used by artists. Jazz and chamber music concerts are popular on Sundays, and the museum also provides a wide variety of art-related programs for children. This is a great place for families, especially on weekends.

Schomburg Center for Research in Black Culture (Manhattan, Harlem)

Branch of New York Public Library
515 Malcom X Boulevard
at West 135th Street
New York, New York 10037
(212) 491-2200

Open: Daily; Exhibition hours Monday, Tuesday, Wednesday 12–8; Friday–Saturday 10–6; Sunday 1–5; Group tours by appointment. Call (212) 491-2229.

Closed: Major holidays

Entry fees: Yes

Type: African history, culture, arts

Subway: 7th Avenue 2, 3 to 135th Street

Bus: M7, M100 to 135th Street

Museum shop: Yes

Restaurant: No

Disabled Access: Yes

The center is named for Arthur A. Schomburg, a Puerto Rican of African descent who migrated to the United States at the turn of the century. Over his lifetime he collected, interpreted, and preserved thousands of books, original manuscripts, and works of art on the history of Africans and their descendants. His amassed collection was eventually donated to the New York Public Library and became the core of what is now the world's largest and finest research center of its kind. Today you'll find more than five million items—rare books, manuscripts, photographs, original sheet music, fine art, and audiovisual materials. A new facility opened in 1991 to accommodate this large and ever-evolving collection. State-of-the-art technology helps visitors conduct scholarly research on a wide variety of subjects including African history, great literary works, music, and theater. Performances and lectures are offered in a new 350-seat theater. Excellent art exhibitions, many of which travel to other destinations, are shown on a regular basis, and a wide variety of educational programs is offered. In addition, more than 400 black newspapers and periodicals from around the world are offered to readers.

Snug Harbor Cultural Center (Staten Island)

1000 Richmond Terrace (Snug Harbor Road and Richmond Terrace)
Staten Island, New York 10301-1199
(718) 448-2500

Open: Wednesday–Sunday 12–5 (gallery hours). Grounds open daily during daylight hours. Hours vary according to the areas of the Center. Call ahead.

Closed: Thanksgiving, Christmas, New Year's Day

Entry fees: Entry to the park is free. Suggested donation for entry to the galleries

Type: Art, architecture

Transportation: From the Staten Island Ferry Terminal take the S40 bus to Snug Harbor.

Museum Shop: Yes; open Wednesday–Sunday 1–4:30

Restaurant: Yes; open Tuesday–Friday 11–2 and Saturday–Sunday 12–5

Disabled Access: Yes, but there is limited access to some buildings. Call ahead.

What was formerly a maritime hospital for retired sailors has been transformed into one of America's leading centers for the visual and performing arts. The Cultural Center is located in an 83-acre park, with 28 buildings constructed in a variety of architectural styles including Beaux Arts, Greek Revival, Second Empire, and Italianate. People of all ages can find a wide variety of things to see and do at this bustling center, including art and performance programs for children, lunchtime chats related to architecture, the performing and visual arts, guided tours of the grounds and buildings, and a wide variety of art exhibits and concerts.

Highlights include its latest addition, the **John Noble Collection,** named for the artist whose paintings, sketches, and 5,000 photographs of New York Harbor are featured. Scheduled to open in the near future is a newly restored 800-seat theater, the second-oldest theater in New York City (only Carnegie Hall is older), where year-round concerts, dance and theatrical productions are held. The **Newhouse Center for Contemporary Art** features changing exhibitions of contemporary art and an annual outdoor summer sculpture exhibition.

Also located at Snug Harbor is the **Staten Island Children's Museum,** the **Staten Island Botanical Garden, The Art Lab** (an art school), artists' and musicians' studios and many nonprofit organizations.

The Society of Illustrators Museum of American Illustration (Manhattan, Upper East Side)

128 East 63rd Street (between Park and Lexington Avenues)
New York, New York 10021
(212) 838-2560
Open: Tuesday 10–8;
Wednesday–Friday 10–5;
Saturday 12–4

Closed: Sunday, Monday, most holidays
Entry fees: Free
Type: Art, specializing in illustration
Subway: B, Q, 4, 5, 6, N, R
Bus: M1, M4, M101, M102, Crosstown M30
Museum Shop: Yes
Restaurant: No
Disabled Access: Only to ground-level gallery

This is the only national institution whose members are professional artists in the fields of illustration, cartooning, animation, and graphic design. For a pleasant change of pace from other art museums, the Society presents exhibitions that feature works created by those talented folks who illustrate greeting cards, children's books, cartoons, print advertising, magazines, posters, and more.

✳ Staten Island Institute of Arts and Sciences (Staten Island)

75 Stuyvesant Place
Staten Island, New York 10301-1998
(718) 727-1135
Open: Daily. Monday–Saturday 9–5; Sunday 1–5
Closed: Most public holidays. Call ahead for information.
Entry fees: Suggested donation
Type: Art, science, history, natural history
Transportation: Staten Island Ferry to St. George Terminal. Walk two blocks to Wall Street, turn left. Follow Wall Street one block to the Institute.
Museum Shop: Yes
Restaurant: No
Disabled Access: Yes

Few museums offer as much in the way of variety as does the Staten Island Institute of Arts and Sciences. Its collection is both eclectic and large, with over two million artifacts that include a natural history collection of 500,000 insects (300,000 of which make up the beetle collection alone!), 25,000 plant specimens, shells, and a variety of archaeological specimens. The art collection spans thousands of years, from ancient to contemporary times. Local artists such as Jasper Cropsey and Jean Pene du Bois are well-represented, as well as American and international superstars such as Marc Chagall, Reginald Marsh, and Robert Henri. Activities offered are numerous, including walking tours, lectures, and educational forums. You'll always be able to see rotating exhibitions on a wide variety of subjects including art, decorative arts, design, antique furniture, silver, and subjects on the natural and cultural history of Staten Island. Call ahead for a current schedule of special activities and exhibitions.

Staten Island Ferry Collection of the Staten Island Institute of Arts and Sciences

St. George Ferry Terminal
Staten Island, New York
(718) 727-1135

Open: Daily. Monday–Friday 10–3; Saturday 10–4; Sunday 11–4

Closed: Major holidays

Entry fees: Yes

Type: History

Transportation: Staten Island Ferry

Museum Shop: Yes

Restaurant: Yes. Food facilities in terminal and surrounding area

Disabled Access: Yes

An entertaining and informative exhibition celebrates the world's most famous commuter ferry through memorabilia, scale models, and historic photographs. Commuters, old and new, should stop here at least once.

Statue of Liberty

Liberty Island, New York Harbor
New York, New York 10004
(212) 363-8828
(212) 269-5755 (ferry information)

Open: Daily 9:30–5, with extended hours during the summer

Closed: Christmas

Entry fees: Free. The only cost to see the Statue of Liberty and Ellis Island is the fee for the boat ride. However, donations are gratefully accepted.

Type: American history

Subway: 1, 4, 5, 9, N, R to Battery Park, then take Circle Line Ferry.

Bus: M1, M6, M15 to Battery Park, then take Circle Line Ferry.

Museum Shop: Yes

Restaurant: Yes. Light refreshments

Disabled Access: Yes. Not available to the crown, which requires many steps to reach

It's always a thrill when you first spot the Statue of Liberty standing majestically in the New York City Harbor, with her torch held high, welcoming Americans and foreigners alike.

Liberty draws more visitors than almost any other major monument in America. She stands 305 feet, 1 inch high from pedestal foundation to the tip of the torch, and was at one time the tallest structure in New York. The length of her right arm alone is 42 feet (it's the one that carries the torch), her hand is 16 feet long, her index finger is a lengthy 8 feet and she weighs in at 225 tons. At the base of the statue is a museum where visitors can see displays about its history. Take the elevator to the viewing platform at the top of the pedestal to experience unparalleled views of the harbor and New York's skyline. Walk up another 12 stories to her crown, and the views are even more spectacular. A visit to the Statue of Liberty is well worth the trip and will surely inspire feelings of pride and patriotism. Your excursion should also include a visit to Ellis Island.

On a bronze tablet affixed to an interior wall of the pedestal is the poem "The New Colossus," written by Emma Lazarus in 1903 to help raise funds for the statue's pedestal. It has become synonymous with the Statue of Liberty herself, and the hope for freedom and opportunity that she represents. It reads:

"Give me your tired, your poor, your huddled masses yearning to breathe free, The wretched refuse of your teeming shore, send these, the homeless, tempest-tossed to me: I lift my lamp beside the golden door."

Studio Museum in Harlem (Manhattan, Harlem)

144 West 125th Street (between Lenox and 7th Avenues)
New York, New York 10027
(212) 864-4500

Open: Wednesday–Friday 10–5; Saturday–Sunday 1–6

Closed: Monday, Tuesday

Entry fees: Yes

Type: Art

Subway: 2, 3 to 125th Street/ Lenox Avenue

Bus: M2, M7, M10, M101, M102

Museum Shop: Yes

Restaurant: No

Disabled Access: Yes

The award-winning Studio Museum in Harlem is known for presenting outstanding interpretive exhibitions that focus on contemporary and traditional arts of Africa, the African diaspora, Black America, and the Caribbean. The permanent collection includes over 1,500 objects and is divided into three broad categories: 19th- and 20th-century African-American art, 20th-century Caribbean and African art, and traditional African art and artifacts. Well-known black artists represented in the collection include Romare Bearden, Faith Ringgold, Elizabeth Catlett, Melvin Edwards, and Jacob Lawrence.

In addition to two floors of galleries, the museum also has artists' studios, workshops, and a new 5200-square foot sculpture garden.

Ukrainian Museum (Manhattan, East Village)

203 Second Avenue at 12th Street
New York, New York 10003
(212) 228-0110

Open: Wednesday–Sunday 1–5

Closed: Monday, Tuesday

Entry fees: Yes

Type: Art and culture of the Ukraine

Subway: 14th Street/Union Square Station: trains 4, 5, 6; N, R, L trains; Astor Place: train 4; 8th Street Broadway Station: N, R trains

Bus: M15, M101, M102; Crosstown M13, M14

Museum Shop: Yes

Restaurant: No

Disabled Access: Yes

The Ukrainian Museum, one of New York City's most interesting and dynamic new museums, dedicates its energies to preserving the cultural heritage of the large Ukrainian-American community in the city and the nation. Objects of historic or artistic merit pertaining to Ukrainian life and culture are on permanent display. **Highlights** include its outstanding collection of Ukrainian folk costumes, paintings, and sculpture by well-known artists of Ukrainian heritage, woven textiles, kilims, decorative ceramics, brass and silver artifacts, and jewelry. The Museum is noted for its display of colorfully decorated Ukrainian Easter eggs called *psanky*. Educational programs for adults and children include workshops in Ukrainian crafts, Ukrainian Easter egg decoration, lectures, and concerts. Gallery talks are offered for groups by appointment.

* Whitney Museum of American Art (Manhattan, Upper East Side)

945 Madison Avenue
at East 75th Street
New York, New York 10021-2790
(212) 570-3600

Open: Wednesday 11–6; Thursday 1–8 (6–8 free); Friday–Sunday 11–6

Closed: Monday, Tuesday

Entry fees: Yes

Type: American art

Subway: Lexington 4, 5, 6 to 77th Street

Bus: M1, M2, M3, M4; Crosstown M30, M72

Museum Shop: Yes

Restaurant: Yes

Disabled Access: Yes

There's always something exciting going on at the Whitney Museum, whether it's a controversial show such as the recent *Black Male: Representations of Masculinity in Contemporary Art,* the Hopper retrospective, or one of the lively and much-discussed Biennial Exhibitions which are organized every other year to display current trends in art in America.

The collections are housed in a blocky, somber brick building designed by Marcel Breuer. The entrance walkway, which crosses over a sunken moat, enhances the feeling that the building is a sort of modern-day fortress. Once inside, however, the mood changes considerably. You'll find a cheerful light-filled lobby that gives way to small galleries and a stairway down to Sarabeth's

Cafe. Calder's famous wire *Circus,* normally on display in the lobby, is gone temporarily for restoration, but is due to return in the near future. It is in the upstairs galleries that most of the special exhibitions are shown, as well as samplings from the permanent collection.

The permanent collection is impressive, with more than 10,000 paintings, drawings, and sculpture produced solely by American artists. The Whitney Museum also owns the world's most most in-depth collection of work by Edward Hopper as well as 850 paintings and drawings by Reginald Marsh, making it the most significant single collection of his work in the world.

It's impossible to predict what will be on display from the permanent collection, but you may be lucky enough to see several of the following works at any given time. This is the author's wish list of favorites: **Three Flags,** 1958, by Jasper Johns; **My Egypt,** 1927, by Charles Demuth; Edward Hopper's notable **Early Sunday Morning,** 1930; **The White Calico Flower,** 1931, by Georgia O'Keeffe; and **Chinese Restaurant,** 1915, by Max Weber.

Weber, *Chinese Restaurant*

O'Keeffe, *The White Calico Flower*

Whitney Museum of American Art Branch at Philip Morris (Manhattan, Murray Hill)

Philip Morris Building
120 Park Avenue at 42nd Street
New York, New York 10017
(212) 878-2550

Open: Monday–Saturday 11–6;
Thursday 11–7:30

Closed: Sunday

Entry fees: Free

Subway: 4, 5, 6, 7, S to Grand
Central Station/42nd Street

Bus: M4, M5, M104

Museum Shop: No

Restaurant: No

Disabled Access: Yes

A small satellite gallery in corporate
spaces that showcases sculpture
and paintings from the Whitney
Museum's permanent collection.

Science and Specialty Museums

* American Museum of the Moving Image (Queens)

35th Avenue at 36th Street
Astoria, Queens, New York 11106
(718) 784-4520
(718) 784-0077
(program information)

Open: Tuesday–Friday 12–4;
Saturday–Sunday 12–6

Closed: Monday

Entry fees: Yes. Modest extra fee
for celebrity appearances

Type: Specialty/motion pictures,
television, video, and digital media

Transportation: R train to Steinway
Street, use the 34th Avenue exit. Call

travel information line for full details:
(718) 784-4777.

Museum Shop: Yes

Restaurant: Yes

Disabled Access: Yes

The American Museum of the Moving
Image is the only museum in the
country devoted to exploring the art,
history, and technology of the film,
television, and digital media industries.
Located on the grounds of the historic
Astoria Studio complex, just 20 minutes away from midtown Manhattan,
the Museum provides a fascinating
look at how moving images have been
made over the past 100 years.

Highlights: The heart of the
Museum is its core exhibition, *Behind
the Screen*. Two large galleries on the
second and third floors house nearly
1,000 artifacts—everything from
cameras to costumes, zoetropes
to software—and even interactive
experiences that take visitors right
inside the process of making movie
images. The Museum's special exhibitions showcase a permanent collection of more than 70,000 artifacts,
the largest public collection in the
country containing rare photographs,

Hedy Lamarr

personal and business papers, models and miniatures, costumes and wigs, sets, props, cameras, television sets, and commissioned works of art and environments.

Several theaters within the Museum screen more than 500 film, video, and digital media programs annually, from silent films with live musical accompaniment to old Saturday matinee serials and cartoons, to documentaries, to personal interviews with actors, directors, and other key film and television industry professionals.

In this unique environment, even the museum shop is worthy of your attention, with its large selection of books on every aspect of the film, television, and digital media industries and its exclusive line of museum-related merchandise.

Makeup for *Mrs. Doubtfire*

* The American Museum of Natural History (Manhattan, Upper West Side)

See pages 2–17 for detailed information.

* Hayden Planetarium (Manhattan, Upper West Side)

Astronomy Department of the American Museum of Natural History

See pages 16–17 for detailed information.

Note: *The Hayden Planetarium will close in March 1997 for extensive renovations and expansion.*

The American Numismatic Society (Manhattan, Washington Heights)

Audubon Terrace, Broadway at 155th Street
New York, New York 10032
(212) 234-3130

Open: Tuesday–Saturday 9–4:30; Sunday 1–4

Closed: Monday, public holidays

Entry fees: Free

Type: Specialty/history of money. Paper currency, coins, and medals from around the world

Subway: 1 to 157th Street and Broadway; B train to 155th Street and St. Nicholas Avenue

Bus: M4, M5, M101

Museum Shop: Yes

Restaurant: No

Disabled Access: Security will assist, or call ahead to arrange help.

The American Numismatic Society offers a major permanent exhibit that traces the history of money, from all parts of the globe, from ancient times to the present. Here you can learn about the fascinating world of coins, commemorative medals, and paper currency. You'll see the design process for making paper money, learn how coins are minted using various types of metals, and gain an understanding of how coins reflect human history. You can discover how money was produced in ancient times, whose portraits appeared on ancient coins, and learn why coins and commemorative medals are considered important historical resources as well as works of art. The American Numismatic Society also has an internationally recognized research department and library.

✳ Con Edison Energy Museum (Lower Manhattan, East Side)

145 East 14th Street
near 3rd Avenue
New York, New York 10003
(212) 460-6244

Open: Tuesday–Saturday 9–5

Closed: Sunday, Monday

Entry fees: Free

Type: Specialty/history of how energy changed New York City

Subway: L, 4, 5, 6, N; R. Any that go to Union Square.

Bus: Call (718) 330-1234 (New York City Transit Authority travel information).

Museum Shop: No

Restaurant: No

Disabled Access: Yes, via main entrance on Irving Place

This unique museum dedicates itself to Thomas Edison's magnificent invention of electricity with an emphasis on energy sources and their economic and cultural impact on the City of New York.

Highlights include a working model of Thomas Edison's first electrical power plant (located on Pearl Street in Lower Manhattan), and his numerous inventions including the

phonograph and the light bulb. Also on display is a collection of early appliances from the 1890s and 1920s, including antique electric fans, irons, toasters, and refrigerators. You can learn about energy-saving techniques and new product development. One of the most popular attractions is the simulated "walk" beneath a New York street to see all of the utilities in action and how they keep a large city up and running. Electric, steam, water, gas, telephone, and sewer lines light up and help make sense of it all. This is an example of an interactive museum at its best.

✳ U.S.S. *Intrepid* Sea-Air-Space Museum (Manhattan, West Side)

Intrepid Square (at Hudson River)
West 46th Street and 12th Avenue
New York, New York 10036
(212) 245-2533
(212) 245-0072 (information hotline)

Open: Summer (Memorial Day to Labor Day), daily 10–5; Winter (Labor Day to Memorial Day), Wednesday–Sunday 10–5. Ticket booth closes at 4 year-round.

Closed: Monday and Tuesday during the winter season

Entry fees: Yes. Discount to veterans and seniors. Children under 6 free.

Type: Specialty/U.S. Navy aircraft carrier

Subway: All lines to 42nd Street, then crosstown bus M42

Bus: M42

Museum Shop: Yes

Restaurant: Yes. In Technologies Hall area

Disabled Access: Yes, call ahead

The U.S.S. *Intrepid* Sea-Air-Space Museum is an historic 900-foot-long 40,000-ton Essex-class aircraft carrier, the focal point of a complex of seven ships permanently docked in New York City Harbor. She is best known for fighting in key battles during World War II, especially during the Liberation of the Philippines, and various battles during the Vietnam War. The U.S.S. *Intrepid* leaves a legacy of bravery under fire that is legendary, having survived seven bombs, five kamikaze attacks, and one torpedo explosion. So important was her role in the defense of our country, the carrier was designated an historic landmark in 1985, an honor bestowed upon her by the U.S. Department of the Interior.

Intrepid also has the distinction of being used as NASA's prime recovery vessel as part of the Atlantic Fleet. Millions of Americans watched their television sets with fascination when she retrieved Scott Carpenter from his Mercury capsule in 1962, and again in 1965 when she picked up Gus Grissom and John Young from Gemini's "Molly Brown."

Today, *Intrepid* is permanently docked in New York City's harbor, serving an important role as teller of tales to millions of visitors who come aboard to learn about America's history on the high seas, in the air, and in outer space.

Intrepid Sea-Air-Space Museum is a great place for families. You can stroll her decks, learn something about an important part of American military history, see up close an impressive collection of more than 40 aircraft, or merely catch unparalleled harbor views from the ship's bridge. Also on board are changing exhibitions, numerous film and video presentations on a wide range of subjects on wartime remembrances and America's air, sea, and space exploits. Added attractions include guided tours of the submarine, *Growler,* or a visit to the *Edson,* a destroyer where you'll see torpedo rooms, galleys, and top secret missile command areas.

Highlights in the permanent ship collection include the following: aircraft carrier *Intrepid* (open to public); nuclear missile submarine *Growler* (guided tours only); Vietnam War destroyer *Edson* (guided tours only); Coast Guard lightship *Nantucket;* destroyer escort *Slater* (formerly Greece's *Aetos*); research/survey ship *Elizabeth M. Fisher;* and the Coast Guard cutter *Tamaroa.*

Highlights on The Armed Forces Plaza: *Lone Sailor,* sculpture by Felix de Weldon Spencer; *Mast,* from the World War II Coast Guard cutter built in Brooklyn; captured Iraqi tanks; U.S. Army tanks and guns; and recovered shipwreck treasures.

Highlights on *Intrepid's* Flight Deck: The *A-12 Blackbird*, the world's fastest airplane, built to perform CIA super-secret surveillance missions. Capable of mach 3.6, altitudes above 90,000 feet; **Catapult exhibit; Helicopters of Vietnam; AV-8 Harrier** USMC vertical takeoff fighter bomber. On the **Island Decks:** Navigating bridge and captain's sea cabin; flag bridge and admiral's sea cabin; **Spy in the Sky—** special exhibit. **United States Navy Hall:** Missiles, ships, aircraft models, and uniforms, A-4B Skyhawk attack bomber. Panavision war films and Mini-theater presentations. **Intrepid Hall:** Large-scale models of U.S.S. *New Jersey,* U.S.S. *Alaska,* U.S.S. *Intrepid;* **Multimedia presentation, *Spirit of "Intrepid,"*** features largest naval battle in history and kamikaze attacks. **Pioneer Hall:** See an antique biplane, visit the Fisher Gallery, and view war and military subjects in the mini-theater. **Technologies Hall:** Undersea Frontier; *Lunar Landing Module, Intrepid; Gemini capsule reproduction.*

Highlights on *Growler,* Guided Missile Submarine SSG-57 (the only guided missile submarine on public view): **Video presentation; Attack Center;** Missile hangars; **torpedo rooms;** missile guidance center; officers' wardroom; crew's galley; engine rooms.

Museum at the Fashion Institute of Technology (Lower Manhattan)

Seventh Avenue at 27th Street
(southwest corner)
New York, New York 10001-5992
(212) 760-7760
(recorded information)

Open: Tuesday–Friday 12–8;
Saturday 10–5

Closed: Sunday, Monday, legal holidays

Entry fees: Free

Type: Specialty/the world of fashion

Subway: 1 or 9: stop at 28th Street at 7th Avenue; A or E to 8th Avenue

Bus: M10 to 7th Avenue

Museum Shop: Catalogs from past and current exhibitions

Restaurant: No

Disabled Access: Yes, call ahead

If you have an interest in fashion, you'll love the Museum at the Fashion Institute of Technology. Founded in 1967, the Museum is the repository for one of the largest and finest collections of costumes and textiles in the world, dedicated to the documentation of fashion and style in all levels of society.

A mix of contemporary and historical shows, drawn from the museum's collections and from other museums and private sources, interpret the creative process in works of design, fashion, and art and the interrelationships among them. Some exhibitions highlight the history of specific articles of clothing such as lingerie, sportswear, hats, shoes, gloves, and gowns, while others pay tribute to individual fashion designers such as Halston, Balenciaga, and Geoffrey Beene. They reflect and reinforce the wide range of subjects taught at the Fashion Institute of Technology, a college of art and design, business, and technology.

The Museum's collections of costumes, textiles, and clothing accessories are so distinguished and wide ranging that students, historians, fashion designers, and writers the world over come here to do research.

* Museum of Television and Radio (Midtown Manhattan, West Side)

25 West 52nd Street (between
Avenue of the Americas and
5th Avenue)
New York, New York 10019-6101
(212) 621-6800 (daily schedule)
(212) 621-6600 (other information)

Open: Tuesday–Sunday 12–6;
Thursday 12–8; Friday 12–9

Closed: Monday, major holidays

Entry fees: Yes

Type: Specialty/TV and radio

Subway: E or F to 5th Avenue &
53rd Street; N or R to 49th Street
& Broadway; B, D, F, or Q to
Rockefeller Center

Bus: Any southbound buses on 5th
Avenue or Broadway or 7th Avenue.
Any northbound buses on Madison
Avenue or Avenue of the Americas
(6th Avenue)

Museum Shop: Yes

Restaurant: No

Disabled Access: Yes

Have you ever wanted to go back in
history and relive a moment in time,
or watch a special program you once
saw on television? It's possible to do
so when you visit the Museum of
Television and Radio.

There are more than 75,000
radio and television programs in
the archives at this wonderful facility.
Using sound and viewing consoles,
visitors can watch a riveting performance on *Masterpiece Theater*,
chuckle over a favorite Jackie Gleason
comedy sketch, hear Franklin D.
Roosevelt make an impassioned
wartime speech, giggle along with
Lucille Ball on "The Lucy Show,"
or relive an Olympic gold medal
performance.

In addition to the viewing and
listening facilities there are daily
screenings and radio programs,
special galleries that feature
television- and radio-related art
and objects, lectures, seminars,
and other programs that focus
on the business of the television
and radio industries.

The Museum of Television and
Radio is a wonderful alternative for
visitors who want something different from the usual art museum
experience.

* New York City Fire Museum (Manhattan, SoHo)

278 Spring Street
(between Varich and Hudson)
New York, New York 10013
(212) 691-1303

Open: Tuesday–Sunday 10–4;
Thursday 10–9 during June, July,
August

Closed: Monday, legal holidays

Entry fees: Yes

Type: Specialty/firefighting

Subway: C, E, K to Spring Street

Bus: M6, M8, M10 to Spring Street

Museum Shop: Yes

Restaurant: Yes. Soft drinks only, open 4–9 on Thursday during June, July, August

Disabled Access: Yes

Located in a restored firehouse, vintage 1904, this lively museum devotes itself to preserving the history of firefighting in New York City. Over 10,000 visitors come each year to see the museum's fascinating displays of vintage fire equipment and learn about fire safety and prevention. **Highlights** include beautifully preserved horse-drawn and hand-drawn apparatus, antique toys, helmets, protective clothing, photographs, grand silver trumpets (yesteryear's version of loudspeakers) and artwork including a spectacular 9-foot-long oil painting, *Engine Company 81* by Capriano that depicts firemen engaged in fire drill activities. Children and adults love this place.

* New York Hall of Science (Queens)

47-01 111th Street and 46th Avenue (near Shea Stadium, USTA Tennis Center, the Queens Zoo, Queens Museum of Art, and La Guardia Airport)
Flushing Meadows-Corona Park
New York, New York 11368
(718) 699-0005

Open: Wednesday–Sunday 10–5 general public; open exclusively to groups 9:30–2 Monday, Tuesday; groups also Wednesday–Sunday 9:30–5

Closed: Monday, Tuesday to general public, and all major holidays

Entry fees: Yes. Free Wednesday, Thursday 2–5

Type: Science

Subway: 7 Flushing line to the 111th Street Station

Museum Shop: Yes

Restaurant: Yes

Disabled Access: Yes

The New York Hall of Science is New York City's only interactive science and technology museum, and one of its newest. It's located in what was once a pavilion for the 1964–65 World's Fair.

Hands-on exhibits—more than 160 of them, in fact—are everywhere in this exciting and innovative institution. The nice thing about the New York Hall of Science is that it always succeeds in making the learning experience memorable and fun.

Highlights: Imaginative devices encourage participation in such wonderful exhibits as *Seeing the Light*, where visitors explore color, lasers, light and perception; or you can walk through the eye of a needle and feel as tiny as a microbe and learn how unseen microorganisms affect our daily lives as you're introduced to the world's tiniest creatures in *Hidden Kingdoms: The World of Microbes.* If you've ever wondered how atoms work, you can play with a working model of one in the *Atom Exhibition.* And *Sound Sations—The Inside Story of Audio* demonstrates how compact discs, radios, and other sound equipment work. These are only a few of the wonderful activities and displays available to visitors every day. It's no wonder the New York Hall of Science is ranked as one of the top ten science museums in the country.

New York Stock Exchange (Lower Manhattan, Financial District)

11 Wall Street. Visitors Center, 20 Broad Street at Wall Street, 3rd floor
New York, New York 10005
(212) 656-5168
(212) 656-5162
(recorded information)

Open: Monday–Friday 9:15–4

Closed: Saturday, Sunday

Entry fees: Free. Must get entry tickets at 20 Broad Street. Tickets limited.

Type: Specialty/stock market

Subway: 2, 3, 4, 5 to Wall Street; N, R to Rector Street; J, M, Z to Broad Street

Bus: M1, M6, M15

Museum Shop: Yes

Restaurant: No

Disabled Access: Yes

Visitors flock to this institution to see for themselves how America's—and the world's—premier marketplace operates. This can be done by taking a self-guided tour into the Visitors Gallery overlooking the trading floor. A continuous tape explains what's happening, how transactions are made, and describes specific responsibilities of the workers on the floor. There's also a Visitors Center and small museum with interpretive exhibits on the history of the New York Stock Exchange, explanations of the electronic data used, and descriptions of the market's procedures.

Lines form early, and a short waiting period to get into the Visitors Gallery is not unusual.

New York Transit Museum (Brooklyn)

Corner of Boerum Place & Schermerhorn Street
(just over the Brooklyn Bridge)
Brooklyn, New York 11201
(718) 243-5839 (operator)
(718) 694-5102
(recorded information)

Open: Tuesday–Friday 10–4; Wednesday evening until 6; Saturday–Sunday 12–5

Closed: Monday

Entry fees: Yes

Type: Specialty/public transportation

Subway: 2, 3, 4, or 5 train to Borough Hall; A, C, F train to Borough Hall; M, N, R train to Court Street; G train to Hoyt/Schermerhorn

Bus: B25, B26, B37, B38, B41, B52, B61. All stop one or two blocks from museum.

Museum Shop: Yes. Also located at Grand Central Terminal and Penn Station in Manhattan.

Restaurant: Yes. Lunch room area on premises but visitors must bring their own food.

Disabled Access: Yes

Housed in an original subway station built in 1936, this pleasant theme museum tells the story of public transportation in New York City and how it evolved. Here you can learn about the important role public transportation plays in the economic development of a city. The main floor houses an art gallery for changing exhibitions documenting all forms of mass transportation. There is also a vast collection of conveyances on display that encompass everything from horse-drawn carriages to trolleys, elevated railroad cars to early buses and subway cars. **Highlights:** Antique turnstiles, architectural drawings of subway systems, stations, antique trains with wicker seats, and the original "A" Train, immortalized by Duke Ellington. Activities and programs including tunnel tours, lectures, and courses on all aspects of the history of mass transit are ongoing. Call ahead for current information.

South Street Seaport Museum (Lower Manhattan, Financial District)

East River at Piers 15 and 16, South Street, Front Street, Water Street, St. John Street, and Fulton Street
New York, New York 10038
(212) 748-8600

Open: Daily 10–6 (May–September); Daily 10–5 (October–April)

Closed: Some public holidays. Call ahead.

Entry fees: Yes

Type: Specialty/nautical, ships, history of seaport

Subway: 2, 3, 4, 5, J, Z, or M to Fulton Street; A and C to Broadway-Nassau; E to World Trade Center, walk east on Fulton to Water Street

Bus: M15

Museum Shop: Yes, plus many other kinds of shops throughout the complex

Restaurant: Yes, there are many eateries throughout the complex.

Disabled Access: Partial; only one gallery is accessible.

The South Street Seaport Museum is located at the southern end of Manhattan, very close to the Brooklyn Bridge. It is an 11-square-block complex that incorporates restored 19th-century buildings that are now used to showcase New York's history as a major world seaport. This lively center teems with activity year-round, with over 10 million visitors enjoying its many shops and restaurants, on-board boat tours, cruises, films, and numerous other activities. It is also from here that the renowned annual Mayor's Cup Race occurs, one of New York City's best-known annual events.

The nautical museum is made up of several components: the Whitman and Melville Exhibition Galleries, The Children's Center (165 John Street), a working 19th-century print shop, and a maritime crafts center.

Highlights: Be sure to visit the lightship *Ambrose,* and look in on the museum's unsurpassed collection of ship models at the Whitman Gallery.

Children's Museums

* The Brooklyn Children's Museum (Brooklyn)

145 Brooklyn Avenue
at St. Mark's Avenue
Brooklyn, New York 11213
(718) 735-4400

Open: Wednesday–Friday 2–5; Saturday–Sunday 12–5

Closed: Monday, Tuesday

Entry fees: Yes. Suggested donation

Type: Specialty/activities for children and their families

Subway: 3 to Kingston Station

Bus: Bus from Manhattan to connect with the B45 or B65 in Brooklyn

Museum Shop: Yes

Restaurant: Yes

Disabled Access: Yes

Because The Brooklyn Children's Museum was the first of its kind in the world, it has served as the definitive model for other children's museums over the past century. From its beginning, the museum placed an emphasis on having participatory exhibits, believing that children learn best through firsthand experience. It has a unique collection of over 27,000 cultural artifacts and natural history specimens plus a collection of live plants and animals. Its exhibits have won numerous awards.

There's always something exciting going on here: hands-on scientific exhibits, theatrical performances, exploring and learning about plants and animals, art and music workshops, learning experiences about other cultures and customs, plus a wide variety of family activities. Everyone has a great time and leaves feeling happy.

* Children's Museum of Manhattan (Manhattan, Upper West Side)

The Tisch Building
212 West 83rd Street (between Broadway and Amsterdam Avenue)
New York, New York 10024
(212) 721-1234

Open: Summer (July 1 to Labor Day): Wednesday–Monday 10–5; Winter (Labor Day to June 30): Monday, Wednesday, Thursday 1:30–5:30; Friday–Sunday 10–5

Closed: Tuesday, major holidays
Entry fees: Yes
Type: Children (toddlers through age 12)
Subway: 1, 9, B, C, E
Bus: M10, M11, M27, M28, M104
Restaurant: No
Museum Shop: Yes
Disabled Access: Yes

Travelers with children take note: if you're tired of hearing the kids complain that "there's nothing fun for us to do," the Children's Museum of Manhattan is just the place for you. Youngsters, from toddlers to early teens, will love the numerous ongoing activities, and the nice thing is that almost all of the displays and play areas are participatory.

In this stimulating environment children's imaginations, curiosity, social skills and learning skills are strengthened. Here they are welcome to participate in a wide variety of activities ranging from creating their own museum masterpieces to clay modeling, painting, and drawing. They can learn to recognize various sounds made by musical instruments and experience performances by professional artists in dance, music, theater, and puppetry. Some activities involve storytelling or playing with other children in a kid-size grocery store. Children can even pretend to be a television newscaster in the Time Warner Media Center.

CMOM is an evolving center for play and learning; therefore its exhibits change from time to time. However, the goals remain the same, and you can be certain that whatever the changes may be, they will be fun, stimulating, and educational for one and all.

Highlights: **Soundsfun:** Use a computer to create sounds and rhythms made by percussion instruments. Maira Kalman's **Max, A Dog:** A tail-wagger who creates poetry as kids learn through his words, images, and sounds. **Time Warner Media Center:** Children learn how to produce and participate in a TV program in CMOM's professional television studio. They can choose to be a newscaster, camera operator, actor, or director. **Helena Rubinstein Literacy Center:** Teachers, parents, and children come here to listen to storytellers or just read quietly. **Sussman Environmental Center:** Learn how to care for our environment. Experience how cities deal with problems relating to water, garbage, plant life in the **Outdoor Urban Tree House** exhibition. **Early Childhood Center:** Bring the little ones, age four and under, to crawl, run, touch, climb, paint, and read books in a happy and safe environment. Theater: See special performances and meet professionals in dance, theater, music, and puppetry. **Russ Berrie Art Studio:** If you want to create your very own masterpiece, this is the place to be. Teachers and artists are on hand to help guide and encourage the creative processes. **Family Learning Center:** Run a grocery store, explore a sandcastle, participate in family art and music workshops.

Children's Museum of Manhattan, play area

* **Staten Island Children's Museum (Staten Island)**

1000 Richmond Terrace,
at the Snug Harbor Cultural Center
Staten Island, New York 10301-9926
(718) 273-2060

Open: Tuesday–Sunday 12–5

Closed: Monday, major holidays

Entry fees: Yes. Entry to park is free. Free for children under 2 years (no strollers allowed in museum)

Type: Children's activities, many hands-on science-related projects

Transportation: From the Staten Island Ferry Terminal take the S40 bus to Snug Harbor.

Museum Shop: Yes

Restaurant: Not within the museum but there are cafe/restaurant facilities within the Snug Harbor complex

Disabled Access: Yes

This highly acclaimed children's museum makes learning fun for kids of all ages through award-winning programs that provide hands-on experiences with themes from the world of science, art, and the humanities. From the moment you enter, the excitement begins to happen. As an example, suspended in the atrium above the reception area a six-foot-long kinetic porpoise arches his tail and snaps his jaw in pursuit of minnows destined to elude him. And this is just for openers. Kids love the **Third Floor Gallery,** a total environment for learning about scale, texture, geometry, pattern, and simple technology. Children's bodies become part of the art as they climb every which way around the exhibition's large sculpture. **Wonder of Water** teaches visitors what water is, what it does, how it's used, and what can be done to keep it fresh and flowing in our environment. **Block Harbor** provides space for the youngest visitors and their families to interact socially and develop cognitive skills; it's set in a harbor scene complete with pirate ship, a vast collection of blocks, and a menagerie of animal toys. **Bugs and Other Insects** is a crawl-in, kid-scaled ant home where youngsters learn about the miniature world of insects.

Historic Houses

Abigail Adams Smith Museum (Manhattan, Upper East Side)

421 East 61st Street
near First Avenue
New York, New York 10021
(212) 838-6878

Open: Monday–Friday 12–4; Sunday 1–5 from September to May. Tuesday until 8 in June and July. City history walking tours on Sundays. Call for complete information.

Closed: Saturday, holidays, and the month of August

Entry fees: Yes. Children under 12 free

Type: History museum

Subway: 4, 5, 6, B, N, R to Lexington Avenue and walk three blocks east

Bus: M15, M31
Museum Shop: Yes
Restaurant: No
Disabled Access: Yes

Constructed in 1799, the building originally served as the carriage house of the East River estate planned by Abigail Adams Smith, daughter of President John Adams, and her husband, Colonel William Stephens Smith. Faced with financial difficulties, the Smiths sold the property to William T. Robertson, a wealthy merchant in the China trade, who turned the estate into one of New York's most beautiful showplaces. The property was sold, and the new owners turned the mansion into the Mount Vernon Hotel, an elegant country day resort popular among city residents. When the hotel was destroyed by fire in 1826, all that remained was the stone stable. This building was then remodeled and re-opened for a second time as a hotel. In 1924 the Colonial Dames bought the property, and restored the stone house and gardens to their original splendor. Since 1988 the interpretive focus of the museum has been on the hotel period. The Museum recently installed a 19th-century tavern room and reinstalled the ladies' and gentlemen's parlors to better represent the site as a hotel. The Abigail Adams Smith Museum is one of the few historic sites that illuminate hotel life in the early 19th century.

Nine Federal-period rooms and a colonial revival garden are open for public viewing. **Highlights** include the Ladies' Parlor, a gentlemen's traveling bar, a table made by Joseph Meeks, and Federal and Neoclassical Empire furnishings. Informative walking tours to historic sites in New York City (Sundays) are offered as well as lectures, concerts, and programs for

children. Call ahead for current
schedule.

Alice Austen House
(Staten Island)

2 Hylan Boulevard at Edgewater Street
Rosebank, Staten Island, New York
10305
(718) 816-4506

Open: House open all year,
Thursday–Sunday 12–5;
grounds open daily until dusk

Closed: Monday, Tuesday,
Wednesday, major holidays

Entry fees: Yes

Type: Historic house with gardens

Subway: From Manhattan, take subway to South Ferry (1, 9), Whitehall
Street (N, R), or Bowling Green
Station (4, 5). Take Staten Island Ferry
to Staten Island; from there, bus S51
to Hylan Boulevard. Walk one block
east to house. For car-ferry schedule
call (212) 806-6940.

Bus: From Manhattan, take bus
to South Ferry then follow above
instructions.

Shop: Yes

Restaurant: No

Disabled Access: Yes. Call ahead
for large groups.

This delightful Victorian-style house
is surrounded by lawns and gardens
with a panoramic view of one of New
York's busiest shipping channels, The
Narrows. Built in the 18th century
as a farmhouse, it was expanded and
transformed into a Victorian cottage
by Alice Austen's family and was
home to her for 80 years. It is now
designated as a National Historic
Monument.

Alice Austen was a remarkable
woman, one of America's first female
photographers to record life as she
saw it, honestly and without pre-
tense. She took thousands of pictures

of people, her own house and gardens, views of The Narrows, ships
sailing to and from New York Harbor,
and numerous other subjects that
caught her fancy. **Highlights:** See
sweeping views of The Narrows, the
Manhattan skyline, and the Statue of
Liberty; tour the cozy Austen home,
named "Clear Comfort"; enjoy ongoing photo exhibitions that often
include examples from Austen's
collection of 3,000 negatives.

Bartow-Pell Mansion
Museum Carriage House
and Gardens (Bronx)

895 Shore Road
Pelham Bay Park
Bronx, New York 10464
(718) 885-1461

Open: Wednesday, Saturday, Sunday
12–4. Open for school and group
tours by appointment.

Closed: Monday, Tuesday, Thursday,
Friday. Thanksgiving weekend,
Christmas through New Year's Day.
Gardens open daily except Monday
and major holidays.

Entry fees: Yes. First Sunday of the
month free. Children under 12 free.

Type: Historic house/museum

Subway: 6 Lexington to Pelham Bay
Station; from Pelham Bay take the
45 Westchester Beeline bus to gates.
Bus does not run on Sunday.

Shop: Yes

Restaurant: No

Disabled Access: Limited.
Call ahead.

Escape to 19th-century New York
City as a guest of the Bartows at
their gracious country home. Richly
crafted Greek Revival interiors, furnished in Empire elegance, are com-
plemented by splendid views of the
Delano- and Aldrich-designed formal
gardens.

Bowne House (Queens)

37-01 Bowne Street at 37th Avenue
Flushing, Queens, New York 11354
(718) 359-0528

Open: Tuesday, Saturday, and Sunday
2:30–4:30; visits may be arranged at
other times by appointment.

Entry fees: Yes

Type: Historic house

Subway: 7 train to Main Street,
Flushing

Bus: On Tuesdays take X51; no buses
on the weekend. Also Port Washington line to Main Street, Flushing.

Shop: Yes

Restaurant: No

Disabled Access: Yes

Built by John Bowne in 1661, the
house is an outstanding example
of Dutch-English architecture. It
stands out as one of New York's
historic points of interest, for it was
here that John Bowne vociferously
opposed New Amsterdam Governor
Pieter Stuyvesant's attempts to out-
law the Quaker sect. A century later,
his arguments became a cornerstone
of the First Amendment to the Constitution, which guarantees every
American citizen religious freedom.
Highlights include a collection of
17th- and 18th-century furniture,
paintings, artifacts, and Bowne
family documents.

Conference House (Staten Island)

7455 Hylan Boulevard
near Satterlee Street
Staten Island, New York 10307
(718) 984-6046

Open: May to November 12th only:
Friday–Sunday 1–4

Closed: Remainder of the year

Entry fees: Yes

Type: Historic house

Transportation: Via car, exit
Verrazano Narrows Bridge at Hylan
Boulevard, continue to end.

Shop: Yes

Restaurant: No

Disabled Access: No

This historic manor house is located
in the 226-acre Conference House
Park at the southern tip of Staten
Island. Built of fieldstone in the pre-
Revolutionary period, circa 1670,
the home was formerly a part of the
much larger 1600-acre Billop Manor
estate which was used as the site for
the Staten Island Peace Conference
in 1776. A defining moment in
American history occurred here
when Benjamin Franklin and John
Adams made it very clear to the
English representatives that the
Colonies wanted their independence.
The declaration of war by the
American patriots against England
came shortly afterward. **Highlights**
include 18th-century furniture and
gardens. Activities include art exhibitions, concerts, lectures, and crafts
workshops.

Dyckman Farmhouse Museum (Manhattan, Upper West Side)

4881 Broadway (at 204th Street)
New York, New York 10034
(212) 304-9422

Open: Tuesday–Sunday 11–4; call
ahead for Sunday hours during winter
(Labor Day–Memorial Day) as these
hours may vary.

Closed: Monday, major holidays

Entry fees: Free. Donations
appreciated

Type: Historic house

Subway: A train to 207th
Street/Washington Heights

Bus: M100

Museum Shop: No

Restaurant: No

Disabled Access: No

Because of its strategic location in the upper reaches of Manhattan, this Dutch-American house was a key place of refuge for the militia during the American Revolutionary War. It was occupied at various times by both the British and the Continental armies. The home was rebuilt in 1784 after it was destroyed by fire.

Highlights include relics from the Revolutionary War, and six rooms with Early American furniture. Activities include concerts, lectures, poetry readings, and crafts demonstrations.

Edgar Allan Poe Cottage/Bronx County Historical Society (Bronx)

Poe Park, Grand Concourse, and East Kingsbridge
Bronx, New York 10458
(718) 881-8900

Open: Saturday 10–4; Sunday 1–5. Group tours can be scheduled by appointment at other times.

Closed: Monday–Friday, major holidays

Entry fees: Yes

Type: Historic house

Subway: D train to Kingsbridge Road

Bus: BX1, BX2, BX34, BX12, BX28, BX26, BX9, BX24, BX32, BX15, BX41, BX55, BX22. Ask for the nearest stop where you may easily proceed to Grand Concourse and East Kingsbridge Road. From Manhattan, Liberty Lines Madison Avenue-Grand Concourse Express 4A and 4B to Kingsbridge Road.

Shop: Yes

Restaurant: No

Disabled Access: No

Poe fans will enjoy making a pilgrimage to this modest cottage, the poet's last home. While Poe's wife was struggling against tuberculosis, it was here that he wrote numerous works including his famous "Annabel Lee." The cottage was moved from its original site in the Bronx to Poe Park in 1913 and the Bronx County Historical Society restored it to look as it did when Poe lived there.

Highlights include ongoing exhibits reflecting the life and times of Edgar Allan Poe, a film about Poe's life and literary career, and a variety of cultural events. Call ahead for current information.

Garibaldi-Meucci Museum (Staten Island)

420 Tompkins Avenue
Staten Island, New York 10305
(718) 442-1608

Open: Tuesday–Sunday 1–5, guided tours

Closed: Monday, major holidays

Entry fees: Contribution requested

Type: Historic house

Transportation: Take Staten Island Ferry, then bus S52, S78, or S79 to Tompkins Avenue

Museum Shop: No

Restaurant: No

Disabled Access: Yes

At varying times between 1850 and 1889, two Italian immigrants of great renown lived in this modest home. Antonio Meucci, the original inventor of the telephone, was its first occupant and later, the great Italian patriot Giuseppe Garibaldi took up residence as the guest of Meucci from 1850–1854. Thanks to the Sons of Italy in America, the home is maintained as a memorial to the lives of both these men for their contributions to society.

Antonio Meucci's great invention, the transmission of the human voice over electrical wires, occurred years before Alexander Graham Bell patented the telephone. Although Meucci filed for the preliminary patent, illness, personal problems, and financial reverses prevented him from renewing his legal rights to his invention. In 1876, when Alexander Graham Bell secured his telephone patent, Meucci and his friends sought prior claim through the courts, but lost their suit. Meucci died without rights to his invention or the recognition that went with it.

Meucci's friend, Giuseppe Garibaldi, took refuge here when he was forced to flee his home in 1850 during the war for the unification of Italy. He later returned to his homeland, fought on for his cause, and achieved great fame for victories that ultimately achieved Italy's goal to become a unified country.

Highlights: Downstairs look for the death mask of Meucci, a rocking chair made of tree branches, and photos that document the transformation of the home to a museum. Upstairs is a re-creation of the room in which Giuseppe Garibaldi lived. There is also a research library, and programs on Italian-American heritage are offered to the public.

Gracie Mansion (Manhattan, Upper East Side)

At Carl Schurz Park
East End Avenue at 88th Street
New York, New York 10128

Open: Tours Wednesday by appointment only

Closed: Remainder of the week

Entry fees: Suggested donation

Type: Historic house

Subway: 4, 5, or 6 train to 86th and Lexington

Bus: 86th Street crosstown bus

Museum Shop: Yes

Restaurant: No

Disabled Access: Yes

Fine and decorative art fill this beautiful Federal-style frame building, built in 1799 for Archibald Gracie, a wealthy Scottish-born sea merchant. Now restored to its original splendor, Gracie Mansion serves as the official residence of the Mayor of New York City. The home has been the site of numerous important meetings and civic events, and serves as a pleasant setting for entertaining presidents, prime ministers, and celebrities from all walks of life.

Its first occupant was Mayor Fiorello La Guardia, who resided here from 1942 to 1945. Since then, eight mayors have occupied the mansion.

Each room is graced with notable antiques and works of art. If you've been lucky enough to tour the mansion, you can extend the pleasure by strolling through Carl Schurz Park which surrounds the building and opens out onto the John Finley Walk which trails along the East River.

Kingsland House/ Queens Historical Society (Queens)

143-35 37th Avenue
Flushing, Queens, New York 11354
(718) 939-0647

Open: Daily. Call ahead for daily schedule and times for tours.

Entry fees: Yes, for tours

Type: Historic house

Subway: 7 to last stop, Main Street, Flushing. Proceed two blocks east on Roosevelt Avenue to Bowne

Street. Turn left, proceed to Margaret Carman Green Park, walk through it, and Kingsland House/Queens Historical Society is the first house on the left.

Bus: Q13 or Q28 to Parsons and Northern Boulevards. Q12, 14, 15, 16, 17, 20, 26, 27, 28, 44, 48, 65, 66 to Main Street, Flushing, and follow above subway instructions.

Shop: Publications only

Restaurant: No

Disabled Access: First floor only

Kingsland House is a colonial farmhouse built by Benjamin Doughty in 1785. It takes its name from his son-in-law, sea captain Joseph King who bought the home in 1801. Today the building serves as headquarters for the Queens Historical Society.

The first floor has special exhibits, while the second floor parlor is decorated with original Victorian furnishings and Doughty family memorabilia. Among the activities offered by the Queens Historical Society are walking tours of Queens, New York City's largest borough, and lectures and slide shows relating to the history of Queens. It also serves as a local research history center. Call ahead for information.

Lefferts Homestead (Brooklyn)

Empire Boulevard off of Flatbush Avenue near the Willink Entrance to Prospect Park
Brooklyn, New York 11215
(718) 965-6505 or (718) 965-8988

Open: Hours change seasonally. Call ahead for update.

Entry fees: Free

Type: Children's historic house/museum

Subway: D, Q

Bus: B41, B48

Shop: Yes

Restaurant: No

Disabled Access: Wheelchair ramp to first floor

This sturdy home is an outstanding example of Dutch Colonial architecture combined with early Federal-style details. It has a high bell-shaped roof (with space beneath to house a smoke-room), a typical split Dutch door at its entry, and long front and back porches with overhangs supported by slender columns.

Peter Lefferts, a well-to-do landowner, had the house built in 1783. Four generations of the Lefferts family lived on the homestead until it was purchased by the City of New York in 1918 and moved a short distance to the present site.

Highlights: There are "reproduction period rooms" in which children can play and imagine themselves living in the past. These include a kitchen, workshop, and the bedrooms of Dutch, African and Native American (Lenape) children. Reproductions, including one of a modern spinning wheel, are used for crafts demonstrations and other hands-on activities. The parlor and grandmother's room are furnished with Federal-style antiques that reflect family life at the homestead in the early 1800s. Look for an 18th-century spinning wheel, a mural that children can color and a dollhouse model of the homestead. Special programs offered throughout the year include changing exhibitions, crafts demonstrations, and lectures.

Morris-Jumel Mansion (Manhattan, Harlem/ Washington Heights)

65 Jumel Terrace between 160th and 162nd Streets (Roger Morris Park)
New York, New York 10032
(212) 927-2533

Open: Wednesday–Sunday 10–4

Closed: Monday, Tuesday, July 4th, Thanksgiving, Christmas, New Year's Day

Entry fees: Yes

Type: Historic house/museum

Subway: B to 163rd Street (weekdays); C to 163rd Street (weekends)

Bus: M2 (Madison Avenue) to 160th Street and Edgecombe Avenue (walk uphill one block); M3 or M18 to 160th Street and St. Nicholas Avenue; M101 to 160th Street and Amsterdam Avenue

Shop: Yes

Restaurant: No

Disabled Access: Yes

Recently restored to its original condition, the Morris-Jumel Mansion is the oldest remaining house in Manhattan and is listed on the National Register of Historic Places. The home was used as George Washington's headquarters in New York until October of 1776, and later became a tavern where Washington stopped with cabinet members in 1790.

Stephen Jumel bought the mansion and settled there with his wife, Eliza Bowen. After his death, Eliza then married ex-Vice President Aaron Burr in the parlor of this home. The marriage was short-lived, but many of Burr's items remain as a reminder of that time. **Highlights** include an octagonal drawing room and Early American furnishings that reflect its past history.

Old Merchant's House (Manhattan, East Village)

29 East Fourth Street
(between Bowery and Lafayette)
New York, New York 10003
(212) 777-1089

Open: Sunday–Thursday 1–4

Closed: Friday, Saturday

Entry fees: Yes

Type: Historic house

Subway: 6, A, B, C, D, E, F, K, RR

Bus: M1, M5, M6, M102

Shop: No

Restaurant: No

Disabled Access: No

Enter this time capsule located just off Washington Square and feel transported back to a time when life was gentler. Two generations of the Seabury Tredwell family lived here from 1835 until the last member of the family died in 1933.

The house was built by Joseph Brewster in 1832, and bought three years later by Seabury Tredwell, a wealthy hardware merchant. The building has a late Federal-style exterior, a Greek Revival interior, and is complete with original furniture and Tredwell family memorabilia including clothing and accessories. **Highlights:** The parlor on the main floor features a portrait of Tredwell over a horsehair sofa, and a painting of his wife over the piano. The parlor carpeting is a reproduction of a French moquette in crimson and gold, circa 1870. In the kitchen is an antique cast-iron stove and a beehive oven, and upstairs, in the Tredwell's bedroom, there are tester beds, as well as period gowns and accessories displayed in glass cases.

Theodore Roosevelt Birthplace National Historic Site (Manhattan, Murray Hill)

28 East 20th Street (between Broadway and Park Avenue South) New York, New York 10003 (212) 260-1616

Open: Wednesday–Sunday 9–5; guided tours hourly between 10 and 4.

Closed: Monday, Tuesday, and all federal holidays

Entry fees: Yes. Children under 17 and senior citizens free

Type: Historic house

Subway: 6, N, R

Bus: M1, M2, M3, M5, M6, M7

Restaurant: No

Shop: Yes

Disabled Access: No

This handsome brownstone is a reconstruction of the original home in which President Theodore Roosevelt was born and lived until he was fourteen years old. You'll see personal memorabilia, photos, family documents, furnishings, and period rooms decorated in styles fashionable between 1865 and 1872.

Highlights: Theodore Roosevelt's Rough Rider uniform, a shirt with the bullet hole from a 1912 assassination attempt, first editions of all 40 of the books written by the President, and a stuffed lion that recalls his expertise as a hunter.

Van Cortlandt House (Bronx)

Van Cortlandt Park
West 246th Street and Broadway
Bronx, New York 10471
(718) 543-3344

Open: Tuesday–Friday 10–3; Saturday–Sunday 11–4

Closed: Monday

Entry fees: Yes. Children under 12 free

Type: Historic house

Subway: 1 or 9 to 242nd Street/Van Cortlandt Park

Bus: 9 Bronx bus to 242nd Street/ Van Cortlandt Park. Express bus from Manhattan: BX3 to 244th Street (Liberty Line Bus)

Shop: Yes

Restaurant: No

Disabled Access: No

Van Cortlandt House, an elegant three-story fieldstone Georgian mansion built in 1748, is the oldest remaining residence in the Bronx. It's situated in Van Cortlandt Park on land that once was Frederick Van Cortlandt's family plantation. Many military maneuvers were carried out from here during the American Revolution, and it was also from here that George Washington began his victory march into New York City in 1783.

Highlights: Van Cortlandt House is known for its distinguished collection of 17th- and 18th-century Colonial, Dutch, and English furnishings. Many Van Cortlandt family possessions are also on display.

Wave Hill (Bronx)

Independence Avenue and West
249th Street (Riverdale section
of the Bronx)
Bronx, New York 10471
(718) 549-3200

Open: Tuesday–Sunday 9–5:30, and
Fridays until dusk, mid-May to mid-
October; Tuesday–Sunday 9–4:30,
mid-October to mid-May and most
holiday Mondays.

Closed: Monday, Christmas, and
New Year's Day

Entry fees: Yes. Wednesday–Sunday,
children under 6 free

Type: Historic house, emphasis on
natural environment and horticulture

Transportation: 7th Avenue 1 or 9
train to 231st Street; transfer to bus
7 or 10 to 252nd Street, cross Parkway Bridge, turn left, and walk to
Wave Hill Gate

Shop: Yes

Restaurant: Yes

Disabled Access: Partial. Call ahead
for information.

Wave Hill, set in 18 acres of spectacular gardens with views of the
Hudson River, was at various times
home to Mark Twain, Theodore
Roosevelt, and Arturo Toscanini.
Today it functions as an environmental center and botanical garden where
visitors may wander through wooded
paths, stroll through flower, aquatic,
and herb gardens, and visit the conservatory and greenhouse.

Highlights: Art exhibitions are held
in Glyndor House, a 1927 Georgian
Revival building. At Wave Hill House
you'll find the visitors center, cafe,
shop, and a variety of ongoing
activities including concerts, talks

on gardening, land management,
ecology, and more. Wave Hill is a
wonderful alternative to the crowded
streets of Manhattan.

Pieter Claesen Wyckoff House (Brooklyn)

Clarendon Road at Ralph Avenue
Carnarsie, Brooklyn, New York 11210
(718) 629-5400

Open: Summer (May 2–October
31): Thursday–Friday 12–5; Winter
(November 1–May 1): Thursday–
Friday 12–4. Groups by appointment.

Closed: Saturday–Wednesday

Entry fees: Yes

Type: Historic house/museum

Transportation: By car via King's
Highway. By public transportation,
take D or Q train to New Park
Avenue, then take the B8 bus
to Beverly Road and East 59th
Street. The house is one block
from this stop.

Shop: No

Restaurant: No

Disabled Access: Partial. Call ahead.

This charming home was built in
1642 by Pieter Claesen Wyckoff, an
uneducated Dutch immigrant who,
through hard work and determina-
tion, became a successful farmer and
distinguished citizen. Wyckoff House
is said to be the oldest farmhouse in
New York City. It remained in the
family for 250 years.

Modest in size, it still has its original plank floors and wide eaves, and
is surrounded by a garden. This historic house was saved from demoli-
tion in 1952 and restored to its present state. **Highlights:** Furnishings
and objects evoke memories of its
350-year history.

Illustrations

The Cloisters

p. 89: The Cloisters, exterior view

p. 90: (top) Robert Campin (the Master of Flemalle): *Altarpiece of the Annunciation* (The Merode Altarpiece), circa 1425. Oil on wood. Central panel: 25¼" × 24⅞"; Left wing: 25⅜" × 10¾"; Left wing: 25⅜" × 11". Purchase, The Cloisters Collection.

p. 90: (bottom) *The Unicorn in Captivity* (seventh tapestry from the Unicorn Tapestry series), circa 1500. 12 ft. high. Gift of John D. Rockefeller, Jr. 37.80.2, The Cloisters Collection.

p. 91: The Cloisters, interior view

The Frick Collection

p. 94: The Frick Collection, exterior view

p. 95: (left) Jean-Honoré Fragonard, *Love Letters* (from *The Progress of Love*), 1771–73 and 1790–91. Oil on canvas. Approx. 125" high; widths vary. Acc. #15.1.47. Courtesy of the Frick Collection, New York, New York.

p. 95: (right) Rembrandt Harmensz van Rijn, *Self Portrait*, 1658. Oil on canvas. 52⅝" × 40⅞" (133.7 × 103.8 cm). Acc. #6.1.97. Courtesy of the Frick Collection, New York, New York.

The Solomon R. Guggenheim Museum

p. 96: Solomon R. Guggenheim Museum, exterior view

p. 97: (left) Pablo Picasso, *Woman Ironing*, 1904. Oil on canvas. 45¾" × 28¼" (116.2 × 73 cm). Acc. #78.2514 T41. Gift, Justin K. Thannhauser, 1978. Solomon R. Guggenheim Museum, New York.

p. 97: (right) Edgar Degas, *Dancers in Green and Yellow* (*Danseuses vertes et jaunes*), circa 1903. Pastel on paper, mounted on board. 38⅞" × 28⅛" (98.8 × 71.5 cm). Gift, Justin K. Thannhauser, 1978. Solomon R. Guggenheim Museum, New York. Photo: Robert E. Mates © Solomon R. Guggenheim Foundation, New York. FN 78.2514 T12.

Statue of Liberty

p. 112: The Statue of Liberty, distant view

The Whitney Museum of American Art

p. 114: The Whitney Museum of American Art, exterior view

p. 115: (top) The Whitney Museum of American Art, interior view

p. 115: (bottom left) Max Weber, *Chinese Restaurant*, 1915. Oil on canvas. 40" × 48" (101.6 × 121.9 cm) Purchase. Acc. #31.382. The Whitney Museum of American Art.

p. 115: (bottom right) Georgia O'Keeffe, *The White Calico Flower*, 1931. Oil on canvas. 30" × 36" (76.2 × 91.4 cm) Puchase. Acc. #32.26. The Whitney Museum of American Art.

The American Museum of the Moving Image

U.S.S. *Intrepid* Sea-Air-Space Museum

Museum of Television and Radio

Children's Museum of Manhattan

Maps

Unsure of how to get there? You can get help by calling the New York City Transit Authority at the following numbers:

Travel Information: *(718) 330-1234*
General Information: *(718) 330-3000*

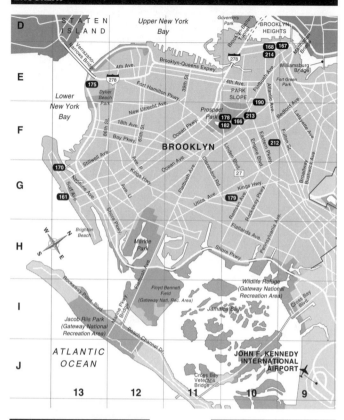

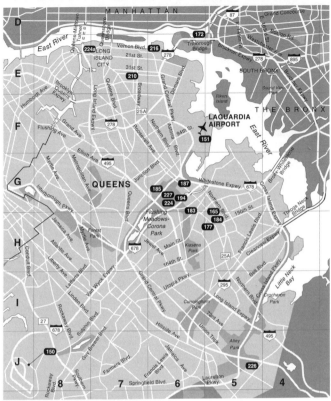

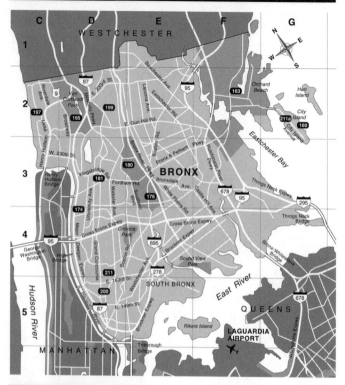

Museums

Historic Houses and Places of Interest

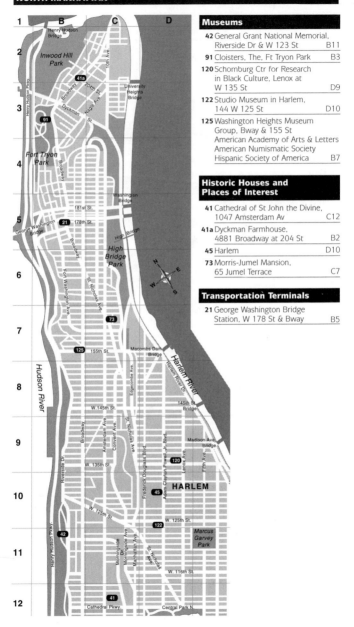

Museums

42 General Grant National Memorial,
Riverside Dr & W 123 St   B11

91 Cloisters, The, Ft Tryon Park   B3

120 Schomburg Ctr for Research
in Black Culture, Lenox at
W 135 St   D9

122 Studio Museum in Harlem,
144 W 125 St   D10

125 Washington Heights Museum
Group, Bway & 155 St
American Academy of Arts & Letters
American Numismatic Society
Hispanic Society of America   B7

Historic Houses and Places of Interest

41 Cathedral of St John the Divine,
1047 Amsterdam Av   C12

41a Dyckman Farmhouse,
4881 Broadway at 204 St   B2

45 Harlem   D10

73 Morris-Jumel Mansion,
65 Jumel Terrace   C7

Transportation Terminals

21 George Washington Bridge
Station, W 178 St & Bway   B5

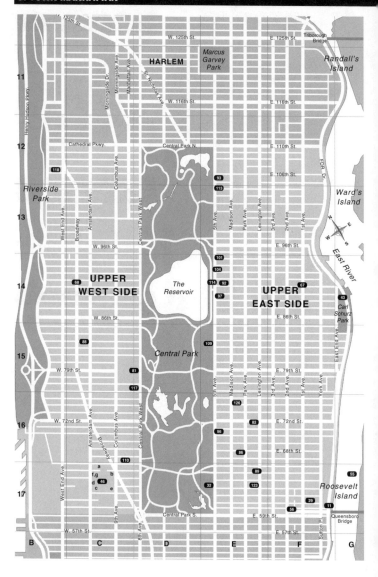

HARLEM

Marcus
Garvey
Park

Randall's
Island

Triborough
Bridge

W. 125th St.

W. 125th St.

E. 125th St.

W. 116th St.

E. 116th St.

11

Henry Hudson Pkwy.

Morningside Dr.

Morningside Ave.

Manhattan Ave.

St. Nicholas Ave.

Cathedral Pkwy.

Central Park N.

E. 110th St.

FDR Dr.

12

118

Riverside
Park

Columbus Ave.

E. 106th St.

Ward's
Island

93

113

5th Ave.

Madison Ave.

Park Ave.

Lexington Ave.

3rd Ave.

2nd Ave.

1st Ave.

13

West End Ave.

Broadway

Amsterdam Ave.

Central Park West

W. 96th St.

E. 96th St.

East River

101

104

UPPER
WEST SIDE

The
Reservoir

114 92

97

UPPER
EAST SIDE

67

43

68

14

W. 86th St.

E. 86th St.

Carl
Schurz
Park

88

109

East End Ave.

Central Park

15

W. 79th St.

81

E. 79th St.

117

5th Ave.

Madison Ave.

Park Ave.

Lexington Ave.

3rd Ave.

2nd Ave.

1st Ave.

York Ave.

Amsterdam Ave.

Broadway

Columbus Ave.

Central Park West

126

16

W. 72nd St.

E. 72nd St.

82

110

96

E. 68th St.

86

a

f,g   b

89

55

d   46   e

Roosevelt
Island

17

c

32

123

29

56

West End Ave.

9th Ave.

8th Ave.

Central Park S.

Central Park S.

11

Sutton Pl.

E. 59th St.

Queensboro
Bridge

W. 57th St.

E. 57th St.

B   C   D   E   F   G

Museums

Historic Houses and Places of Interest

Transportation Terminals

Museums

90	City Gallery, 2 Columbus Cir	D17
90a	Dahesh Museum 601 5 Av at 56 St	E18
90b	Equitable Gallery 787 7th Av at 51st	D18
100	International Center of Photography Midtown, 1133 Av of Americas	D19
102	Intrepid Sea-Air-Space Museum, Hudson River, foot of W46 St	B18
103	Japan Society, 333 E 47 St	F18
103a	Municipal Art Society 457 Madison Av	E18
111	Museum of Modern Art, 11 W 53 St	D18

112	Museum of Television & Radio, 25 W 52 St	E18
119	Pierpont Morgan Library, 29 E 36 St	E20
119a	Rose Museum at Carnegie Hall, 154 W 57 St (2nd Floor)	D18
119b	Sony Wonder Technology Lab. 550 Madison Av at 56 St	E18
129	Whitney Museum of American Art, at Philip Morris: Park Av & E 42 St	E19

Queensboro Bridge

E. 59th St.
E. 57th St.
E. 50th St.
E. 45th St.
E. 42nd St.
E. 38th St.
E. 34th St.
E. 30th St.

Sutton Pl.
Beekman Pl.
FDR Dr.

Queens-Midtown Tunnel

MURRAY HILL

Madison Ave.
Park Ave.
Lexington Ave.
3rd Ave.
2nd Ave.
1st Ave.
Park Ave. S.

103a **103** **66** **65** **15** **34** **10** **129** **119** **16** **17**

E

F

Historic Houses and Places of Interest

Transportation Terminals

Museums

Historic Houses and Places of Interest

Transportation Terminals

* Please note, this is a temporary location.
Call to confirm the museum's address.

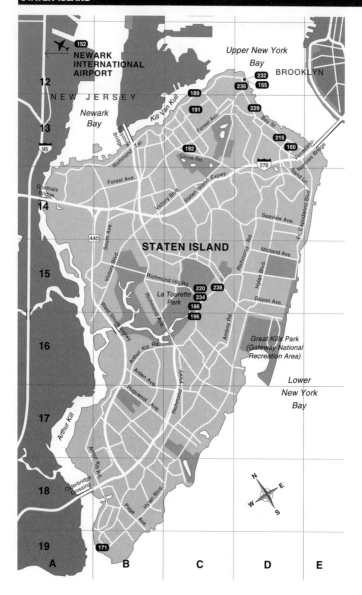

152
NEWARK
INTERNATIONAL
AIRPORT

Upper New York
Bay

BROOKLYN

12

NEW JERSEY

Newark
Bay

13

95

Kill Van Kull

189

191

Forest Ave.

232
155
236

229

Bayonne
Bridge

Richmond Ter.

192

Clove Rd.

Bay St.

215
160

Verrazano-Narrows Bridge

278

Goethals
Bridge

Forest Ave.

14

440

Victory Blvd.

Staten Island Expwy.

Seaview Ave.

Ft. C. Capodanno Blvd.

Richmond Rd.

STATEN ISLAND

15

South Ave.

Victory Blvd.

Richmond Hill Rd.

220
234
238
186
196

La Tourette
Park

Midland Ave.

Hylan Blvd.

Guyon Ave.

16

West Shore Expwy.

Richmond Ave.

Arthur Kill Rd.

Amboy Rd.

Great Kills Park
(Gateway National
Recreation Area)

Lower
New York
Bay

Arthur Kill

17

Arden Ave.

Huguenot Ave.

Richmond Pkwy.

18

Outerbridge Crossing

Arthur Kill Rd.

Page Ave.

Hylan Blvd.

N
W   E
S

19

171

A   B   C   D   E

Types of Collections and Where to Find Them

African-American

Brooklyn Historical Society

The Bronx Museum of the Arts

Ellis Island Immigration Museum

Museum for African Art

Schomburg Center for Research in Black Culture

Staten Island Institute of Arts and Sciences

Statue of Liberty

Studio Museum in Harlem

Americana

The Bronx Museum of the Arts

Dyckman Farmhouse Museum

Edgar Allan Poe Cottage

Ellis Island Immigration Museum

Federal Hall National Monument

Gracie Mansion

Lefferts Homestead

Lower East Side Tenement Museum

The Metropolitan Museum of Art

Museum of American Folk Art

Museum of the City of New York

Museum of Staten Island

The New York Historical Society

Statue of Liberty

Theodore Roosevelt Birthplace National Historic Site

Historic Richmond Town

Abigail Adams Smith Museum

Snug Harbor Cultural Center

South Street Seaport Museum

Art/Africa

The American Museum of Natural History

The Brooklyn Museum of Art

The Metropolitan Museum of Art

Museum for African Art

Art/Ancient Near East

The Brooklyn Museum of Art

The Metropolitan Museum of Art

Art/Far Eastern

The Asia Society Galleries

The Brooklyn Museum of Art

China Institute Gallery

The Frick Collection

Jacques Marchais Museum of Tibetan Art

Japan Society

The Metropolitan Museum of Art

Pierpont Morgan Library

Art/Islamic

The Brooklyn Museum of Art

The Metropolitan Museum of Art

Art/Medieval and Renaissance

The Brooklyn Museum of Art

The Cloisters

The Frick Collection

The Metropolitan Museum of Art

Pierpont Morgan Library

Art/17th and 18th Centuries

The Brooklyn Museum of Art

Dyckman Farmhouse Museum

The Frick Collection

The Metropolitan Museum of Art

Pierpont Morgan Library

Museum of the City of New York

The New York Historical Society

Art/19th and 20th Centuries

American Craft Museum

The Brooklyn Museum of Art

The Bronx Museum of the Arts

City Hall Governor's Room

Federal Hall National Monument

Forbes Magazine Galleries

The Frick Collection

Gracie Mansion

The Solomon R. Guggenheim Museum

The Jewish Museum

The Metropolitan Museum of Art

Morris-Jumel Mansion

Museum of American Folk Art

Museum of the City of New York

The Museum of Modern Art

The New Museum of Contemporary Art

The New York Historical Society

Isamu Noguchi Museum and Gardens

Queens Museum of Art

Schomburg Center for Research in Black Culture

Snug Harbor Cultural Center

Staten Island Institute of Arts and Sciences

Whitney Museum of American Art

Children

The American Museum of Natural History

American Museum of the Moving Image

The Brooklyn Children's Museum

The Brooklyn Museum of Art

The Bronx Museum of the Arts

Children's Museum of Manhattan

Con Edison Energy Museum

Ellis Island Immigration Museum

Forbes Magazine Galleries

Historic Richmond Town

The Solomon R. Guggenheim Museum

The Metropolitan Museum of Art

Museum of the City of New York

Museum for African Art

New York City Fire Museum

The New York Historical Society

Queens Museum of Art

South Street Seaport Museum

Staten Island Children's Museum

Staten Island Institute of Arts and Sciences

Statue of Liberty

Crafts

American Craft Museum

The Brooklyn Museum of Art

Historic Richmond Town

El Museo del Barrio

Museum of American Folk Art

Ukrainian Museum

Decorative Arts
(Ceramics, Furniture, Glass, Silver, Porcelain, Objets d'Art)
American Craft Museum

The Asia Society Galleries

The Brooklyn Museum of Art

City Hall Governor's Room

The Cloisters

Cooper-Hewitt National Design Museum

Dyckman Farmhouse Museum

Federal Hall National Monument

Forbes Magazine Galleries

Fraunces Tavern Museum

The Frick Collection

Gracie Mansion

Hispanic Society of America

Historic Richmond Town

Lefferts Homestead

The Metropolitan Museum of Art

Pierpont Morgan Library

Morris-Jumel Mansion

Museum of American Folk Art

Museum of the City of New York

The New York Historical Society

Old Merchant's House

Edgar Allan Poe Cottage

Theodore Roosevelt Birthplace National Historic Site

Abigail Adams Smith Museum

Staten Island Institute of Arts and Sciences

Egyptian Art
The Brooklyn Museum of Art

The Metropolitan Museum of Art

Fashion, Costumes
The Brooklyn Museum of Art

The Metropolitan Museum of Art

Museum at the Fashion Institute of Technology

The New York Historical Society

Ukrainian Museum

Gardens
Alice Austen House

Brooklyn Botanic Garden

The Cloisters

Cooper-Hewitt National Design Museum

Dyckman Farmhouse Museum

Gracie Mansion

Historic Richmond Town

Jacques Marchais Museum of Tibetan Art

Morris-Jumel Mansion

The Museum of Modern Art

Isamu Noguchi Museum and Gardens

Abigail Adams Smith Museum

Snug Harbor Cultural Center

Hispanic
Hispanic Society of America

El Museo del Barrio

Judaica
Ellis Island Immigration Museum

The Jewish Museum

Lower East Side Tenement Museum

Libraries

The American Museum of Natural History

The American Numismatic Society

Brooklyn Historical Society

The Frick Collection

Hayden Planetarium

International Center of Photography

The Metropolitan Museum of Art

Pierpont Morgan Library

Museum of Television and Radio

The New York Historical Society

New York Public Library

Schomburg Center for Research in Black Culture

Maritime History

U.S.S. *Intrepid* Sea-Air-Space Museum

Museum of the City of New York

Museum of Staten Island

Snug Harbor Cultural Center

South Street Seaport Museum

Media/Film, Television, Video

American Museum of the Moving Image

International Center of Photography

The Jewish Museum

The Museum of Modern Art

Museum of Television and Radio

Medieval Manuscripts

The Cloisters

The Metropolitan Museum of Art

Pierpont Morgan Library

Photography

Alice Austen House

American Museum of the Moving Image

The Brooklyn Museum of Art

Castle Clinton National Monument

Ellis Island Immigration Museum

Forbes Magazine Galleries

Garibaldi-Meucci Museum

Gracie Mansion

International Center of Photography

The Solomon R. Guggenheim Museum

Lower East Side Tenement Museum

The Metropolitan Museum of Art

El Museo del Barrio

The Museum of Modern Art

The New York Historical Society

Queens Museum of Art

Schomburg Center for Research in Black Culture

Whitney Museum of American Art

Prints and Drawings

Brooklyn Historical Society

The Brooklyn Museum of Art

Cooper-Hewitt National Design Museum

The Frick Collection

The Solomon R. Guggenheim Museum

Hispanic Society of America

The Jewish Museum

The Metropolitan Museum of Art

The Museum of Modern Art

Pierpont Morgan Library

Museum of the City of New York

The New York Historical Society

The Society of Illustrators
Museum of American Illustration

Staten Island Institute of Arts
and Sciences

Whitney Museum of American Art

Science

American Museum of the Moving
Image

The American Museum of Natural
History

Hayden Planetarium

New York Hall of Science

Staten Island Institute of Arts
and Sciences

Sculpture

The Asia Society Galleries

The Brooklyn Museum of Art

The Cloisters

The Frick Collection

The Solomon R. Guggenheim
Museum

Hispanic Society of America

The Metropolitan Museum of Art

El Museo del Barrio

Museum of American Folk Art

Museum of the City of New York

The Museum of Modern Art

Museum for African Art

The New York Historical Society

Isamu Noguchi Museum
and Gardens

Snug Harbor Cultural Center

Statue of Liberty

Whitney Museum of American Art

Textiles

American Craft Museum

The Brooklyn Museum of Art

Cooper-Hewitt National Design
Museum

The Frick Collection

Hispanic Society of America

Historic Richmond Town

The Jewish Museum

The Metropolitan Museum of Art

Museum of American Folk Art

National Museum of the
American Indian

Ukrainian Museum

Victoriana

Alice Austen House

Forbes Magazine Galleries

Museum of the City of New York

The New York Historical Society

Old Merchant's House

Edgar Allan Poe Cottage

Theodore Roosevelt Birthplace
National Historic Site

Appendices

Appendix Contents

Appendix A:

New Museum Listings

Art, science, history and high-tech museums are springing up at an astounding rate throughout America, and New York is no exception. Here are 14 additional museums for your pleasure, with more things to see, experience and enjoy.

* Dahesh Museum
(Manhattan. Midtown)

601 Fifth Avenue
(near 48th Street)
New York, NY 10017
Telephone: (212) 759-0606

Open: Tuesday–Saturday 11–6

Closed: Sunday, Monday

Subway: 6 to 51st and Lexington
Ave; B,Q,D, or F to 47th–50th St.
(Rockefeller Center); 1/9 to 50th St.
& 7th Ave; N or R to 49th &
Broadway

Bus: 1,2,3,4, or 5 downtown to
49th St. & 5th Ave; 1,2,3, or 4
uptown to 48th St. & Madison
Avenue; 5 to 48th and Avenue of the
Americas; 27 or 50 crosstown to
Fifth Ave

Entry Fees: Free

Type: Art

Museum Shop: Yes

Restaurant: No

Disabled Access: Yes

Highlights: This small museum
located in Midtown Manhattan features changing exhibitions, with a
concentration on exquisite examples
of European academic art of the
19th and 20th centuries. Private
collections consist of more than
3,000 works. Activities include
lectures, concerts, gallery talks.

* Dia Center for the Arts
(Manhattan, Chelsea)

548 West 22nd Street (near
11th Ave.) New York, N.Y. 10011
Telephone: 212-989-5912

Open: Thursday–Sunday 12–6

Closed: Monday, Tuesday,
Wednesday, Major holidays

Subway: E or C train near 8th Ave.

Entry Fees: yes

Type: Art, contemporary

Museum Shop: Books

Restaurant: Yes. Coffee bar,
light fare.

Disabled Access: Yes

Dia Center for the Arts presents
changing exhibitions with an emphasis on large-scale, single-artist projects of long term duration (usually
one year). Call ahead for current
exhibition information.

The Equitable Gallery
(Manhattan, Midtown)

787 Seventh Street at 51st
New York, NY
Telephone: (212) 554-4818

Open: Monday–Friday 11–6;
Saturday noon to 5

Closed: Sunday

Subway: A, C

Bus: M10

Entry Fees: No

Type: Fine and decorative arts

Museum Shop: No

Restaurant: No

Disabled Access: Yes

Located in the atrium of Equitable
Tower, this small gallery presents
exhibitions of all fields of the visual
and decorative arts, drawing on collections from within and outside of
New York City. The Equitable Center
also has on display in its public
spaces works by major 20th century
American artists including a spectacularly large painting by Roy
Lichtenstein and works by Sol Lewitt,
Scott Burton, Thomas Hart Benton
and others.

Municipal Art Society (Midtown)

457 Madison Avenue,
between 50th and 51st,
New York, NY 10022
Telephone: (212) 935-3960

Open: Monday–Wednesday;
Friday and Saturday, 11-5

Closed: Thursday, Sunday, Federal holidays

Entry Fees: Yes

Type: Architecture and urban issues for City of New York

Subway: E or F trains to 53rd and 5th Avenue; #6 train to 53rd and Lexington

Bus: M1, M2

Museum Shop: Yes

Restaurant: No

Disabled Access: Yes

Highlights: The Municipal Art Society is situated in a circa 1862 Villard townhouse adjacent to an Italian Renaissance palazzo courtyard that opens onto Madison Avenue (next to the New York Palace Hotel,formerly the Helmsley Palace Hotel). Here visitors can learn about issues pertaining to urban planning, historic preservation, open space and livability issues that effect New York City. Timely exhibitions on local, national and international urban issues are offered as well as guided tours around New York City (by arrangement) and educational programs for all ages.

The Museum of American Financial History (Lower Manhattan, Financial District

24 Broadway at Bowling Green
New York, N.Y.
Telephone: (212) 908-4110

Open: Monday–Friday 11:30–2:30 and by appointment

Closed: Weekends and major holidays

Entry Fees: Free

Type: History of finance in America

Subway: Wall Street 4, 5 and 2,3; Broad Street J,M,Z

Bus: M1, M6, M5

Museum Shop: No

Restaurant: No

Disabled Access: Yes

This is one of the newest museums in New York City, fittingly located in the Standard Oil Building, once the site of the law office of Alexander Hamilton, America's first Secretary of the Treasury. Here you will find historical financial documents, art, and numerous artifacts that trace the history of finance in America through investing, corporate activity, the stock market, and the technological revolution that has changed the way business is conducted from the time of the American Revolution to the present. Among the artifacts on view are engraved stocks and bonds certificates, and a tickertape machine developed by Thomas Edison in 1880.

Museum of Chinese in the Americas (Chinatown)

70 Mulberry Street
at Bayard Street, second floor).
New York, NY.
Telephone: (212) 619-4785

Open: Tuesday–Saturday, 12–5

Closed: Sunday, Monday, major holidays

Entry Fees: Yes. Children under 12 free

Type: History/Chinese heritage

Subway: 4, 5

Bus: 1

Museum Shop: Yes

Restaurant: No

Disabled Access: Call ahead

Focuses on preservation of the Chinese immigrant experience in the Americas. A permanent exhibit, *Where is Home? Chinese in the Americas* explores the immigration of Chinese citizens and their assimilation into Western culture through art, historical interpretation, documents, personal and domestic artifacts, individual stories and common beliefs. Rotating theme exhibits are ongoing. Activities offered include educational walking tours of Chinatown and its historic landmarks.

* Museum of Jewish Heritage, A Living Memorial to the Holocaust (Lower Manhattan, Battery Park City)

18 First Place, Battery Park City, New York, N.Y. 10004-1484
Telephone: (212) 968-1800
Open: Sunday–Wednesday 9–5; Thursday 9–8; Friday and eve of Jewish Holidays, 9–2
Closed: Saturday
Type: History/Judaic
Subway: 1, 9 to South Ferry; N,R to Whitehall; 4,5 to Bowling Green; A, E, C, 2, 3 to World Trade Center
Bus: M1, M6, M9 or M15
Entry Fees: Yes. Senior and student rates. Tickets can be purchased at the door, or by calling Ticketmaster at (212) 307-4007.
Type: Jewish History
Museum Shop: Yes
Restaurant: No
Disabled Access: Yes
Highlights: Located on the waterfront of Battery Park City, the Museum allows visitors to experience the richness of pre-Holocaust Jewish life, the devastation of the Nazi era,

and the hope born of post-war Jewish cultural renewal. The Museum houses a core exhibit of more than 2,000 photographs and 800 historical and cultural artifacts, interspersed with twenty-four original films.

* New York City Police Academy Museum (Manhattan, East Side)

235 East 20th Street between 2nd and 3rd Avenues.
New York, NY 10003
Telephone: (212) 477-9753
Open: Monday–Friday 9–3
Closed: Saturday, Sunday, Federal holidays
Entry Fees: Free
Type: History, New York City Police Department
Subway: 4, 5 or 6
Bus: 101, 102, 103
Museum shop: No
Restaurant: No. Many restaurants in area.
Disabled Access: Yes
Highlights: Come here to learn more about New York City's famous police department. Collections on view include all varieties of police artifacts, guns, ornately carved wooden night sticks, uniforms, handcuffs, photographs and a variety of unusual weapons, all of which date from 1870 to the present, plus examples of antique badges and shields. The museum is housed in the New York City Police Academy building.

North Wind Undersea Institute (Bronx)

610 City Island Avenue,
Bronx, N.Y., 10464
Telephone: (718) 885-0701
Open: Monday–Friday 10–5;

Saturday and Sunday 12–5

Closed: National holidays

Subway: #6 Subway to Pelham Bay Station to the #29 Bus to City Island. First City Island Stop

Entry Fees: Yes

Type: Marine Museum and research center

Museum shop: Yes

Restaurant: No. Many good restaurants are located at the City Island complex

Disabled Access: Yes

Highlights: Hands-on exhibits help visitors learn about marine life and mammals. The collections consist of an extensive shell collection, antique deep-sea diving display, ancient treasures from the deep, and whale rescue equipment. Tours, lectures, activities, and an award-winning video presentation of the historic rescue of Physty the Whale for children and adults. This interesting museum is appropriately situated in a Victorian mansion once owned by a sea captain.

P.S. 1 Contemporary Art Center (Queens)

22-25 Jackson Avenue
at 46th Street
Long Island City (Queens),
New York 11101
Telephone: 718-784-2084

Open: Wednesday–Sunday 12–6

Closed: Monday, Tuesday, major holidays

Entry Fees: Yes. Suggested donation. Reduced rates to seniors and students.

Type: Contemporary art, rotating exhibitions

Subway: From Manhattan take E or F train to 23 St. Ely Avenue; or the #7 to 45 Rd.-Courthouse Square; or the G to Courthouse Square or 21st - Van-Alst

Bus: The Q67 to Jackson and 45th Aves. or the B61 to Jackson Ave.

Museum Shop: No

Restaurant: Yes

Disabled Access: Yes

P.S.1 Contemporary Art Center is located in a 19th century Romanesque-style school building in Long Island City (Queens). It re-opened in the Fall of 1997 following a 3-year reconstruction project. The facility, now greatly expanded and improved, has 125,000 square feet of gallery space, making it one of the largest facilities for contemporary art in the world.

P.S. 1 presents and interprets the work of innovative artists in all media on a rotating basis, and maintains long-term installations by Alan Saret, Richard Serra, James Turrell and Eric Orr. Shows are presented in galleries located througout the building.

Since P.S.1 opened 21 years ago, it has presented over 2,000 exhibitions, surveys and projects both in Long Island City and at the Clocktower Gallery, its affiliate in the Tribeca area of Manhattan, where major artists such as Magdalen Abakanowicz, Michelangelo Pistoletto, Dennis Oppenheim, and Keith Sonnier have been featured.

The Rose Museum at Carnegie Hall (Manhattan, Midtown)

154 West 57th Street
(2nd floor) at 7th Avenue
New York, NY 10019
Telephone: (212) 903-9629

Open: Thursday–Tuesday 11–4:30, and up to half hour before concerts

Closed: Wednesdays, Major holidays

Entry Fees: Free

Type: Theatre Museum

Subway: A, C

Bus: M10

Museum Shop: Yes

Restaurant: No

Disabled Access: Yes

Highlights: Special exhibits and guided tours provide visitors with information about the building's history (circa 1891) and important events that have occured there. On display are artifacts, photographs, posters and playbills from performances at Carnegie Hall by luminaries from the world of opera, symphony, Broadway musicals and more.

Skyscraper Museum (Lower Manhattan, Financial district)

44 Wall Street, New York, N.Y. 10005 **(See note below regarding temporary location)**
Telephone: (212) 968-1961
Open: Tuesday–Friday, 12–6

Closed: Saturday, Sunday, Monday

Entry Fees: Free

Type: Architecture, accent on skyscrapers

Subway: Wall Street 4, 5 and 2,3; Broad Street J,M,Z

Bus: M1, M6, M5

Museum Shop: Yes, small selection of books and posters

Restaurant: No

Disabled Access: Yes

Appropriately located in the Lower Manhattan area, the birthplace of the skyscraper, this new museum keeps it's focus on the highrise structures in New York city. Changing exhibitions will explore all aspects of how skyscrapers are built, why they are important to our economy, and other fascinating topics about these mega structures. **NOTE: The location at 44 Wall Street is TEMPORARY. A permanent home for the** museum will be announced in the near future. Call the number listed above for the exact location.

* Sony Wonder Technology Lab (Manhattan, Midtown)

550 Madison Avenue at 56th Street, between Madison Ave. and 5th Ave.
New York, NY 10022
Telephone: (212) 833-8100
Open: Tuesday–Saturday 10–6; Thursday 10–8; Sunday 12–6

Closed: Monday and major holidays

Entry Fees: Free

Type: Science and Technology, interactive, for visitors of all ages

Subway: 4,5, 6 trains to 59th St; E, F trains to 5th Avenue/53rd Street; or R train to 5th Avenue/60th Street

Bus: M1, M2, M3, M4, M5, M57

Museum Shop: Yes

Restaurant: No. Restaurants in the atrium at the entrance to museum

Disabled Access: Yes

As you arrive you're greeted by *b.b. wonderbot*, the dynamic new telepresence robot. Ask it a question or just carry on a conversation and you'll be amazed by its responses. (A visit to the galleries upstairs will show you why and how *b.b.* can be so smart.) A total of four floors of hands-on interactive exhibits entice visitors to play, particapate, and learn about the wonderful world of of communications technology. Begin by walking into a star-filled sky as you depart the elevator on the fourth floor. Inside you'll be immersed in a century's worth of communications history and technology. Create your personal visitor's card, complete with photo, and begin your tour. Be prepared to be busy with interactive displays as you try your hand at teaching a computer to speak your name, use Cyberplay Online to access CNN, visit popular Internet sites, compose a symphony, or tour the White House with Socks the cat. Everyone, regardless of age, will have great fun exploring this dynamic environment dedicated to the of world science and technology .

Trinity Museum, Trinity Church (Lower Manhattan, Financial District)

Broadway and Wall Streets
New York, N.Y.
Telephone: (212) 602-0800

Open: Monday–Friday 9–11:45 and 1–3:45; Saturday 10–3:45; Sunday 1–3:45

Type: Historic site

Subway: Wall Street 4, 5 and 2,3; Broad Street J,M,Z

Bus: M1, M6, M5

Entry Fees: No

Museum Shop: Yes

Restaurant: No

Disabled Access: Yes

Located in the heart of the financial district, this famous church is amongst the oldest and most beloved in New York City. On display in its small museum are photographs, items of religious significance includ-ing an historic communion plate, drawings and prints. You'll want to browse through the permanent exhibit "The Parish of the Trinity Church in the City of New York: The Evolution of an Urban Institution," which traces the history of the church from the 17th century to the present. Also take note of the com-memorative plate on the entrance steps which proclaims a visit by Queen Elizabeth and Prince Philip.

Appendix B:

What's New

According to a recent survey conducted by the Commerce Department and The Travel Industry of America, museums are now first on tourists' lists of favorite places to visit. To accomodate the huge increase in the numbers of visitors per year, these institutions are refurbishing galleries, expanding exhibition spaces, improving displays, and making things generally more user-friendly. The following infomation provides a brief view of recent changes in New York's major museums.

The American Museum of Natural History.

Galleries now closed for renovations include:

1. The North American Forests Gallery (First Floor). **The Giant Sequoia** (The Mark Twain Tree), featured in Chaper I, page 8, is not presently on view. This gallery is presently closed for refurbishment. Ask at information desk for current status.

2. The Hall of the Biology of Invertebrates (First Floor) is also under renovation. The Giant Mosquito Model, a featured highlight, (see page 8) is presently on view in front of the Information Desk on the First Floor.

3. The Dinosaur Halls have been completed and are fully operational. The displays, in a word, are spectacular. You should begin your tour by viewing the excellent introductory film presented at the Miriam and Ira D. Wallach Information Center on the Fourth Floor, and then proceed to the newly completed Hall of Vertebrate Origins where a Giant Sea Turtle hangs from the ceiling and other fascinating specimens are on display. Also in this area, near the Hall of Saurischian Dinosaurs, be on the lookout for an informative exhibit of the Oviraptor eggs found in Mongolia in 1993 by American Museum of Natural History paleontologists (see page 10 for description).

4. The Hayden Planetarium is now closed and will remain so for several years. It is undergoing total reconstruction and will become the finest museum planetarium in the world.

The Metropolitan Museum of Art

1. The Howard Gilman Gallery, which specializes in photography exhibitions, is now open at the Metropolitan Museum of Art (second floor). Exhibitions will draw on the Gilman Collection of 5,000 works, including rare prints and also from the Metropolitan's own collections and outside sources. Shows will change three times a year.

2. In anticipation of re-opening the **Greek and Roman collections,** the public can get a glimpse of what's to come by visiting the small galleries located along the corridor that approaches the restaurant. The selections from the Greek collection features a *kouros* figure, situated in the center of the gallery, which is surrounded displays of kraters, jewelry and other ethnographic articles of interest. Furthur down the corridor is the Roman Gallery with several spectacular sarcophagi in high relief, plus a charming group of marble heads.

3. New and expanded galleries for **Chinese art** are now open to the public. The renovation occupies spaces on two floors, and doubles the space designated for Chinese art. Four new rooms on the third floor provide a beautiful setting for jades, textiles, ivories and other decorative pieces. Downstairs, (second floor) the spaces have been enlarged to accomodate the reinstallation of 100 paintings and calligraphy. The feeling of uncrowded spaces adds greatly to the pleasure of visiting the Asian collections as a whole.

The Museum of Modern Art
has expanded its hours of operation.
It is now open:

Saturday–Tuesday, 10:30–6; Thursday
& Friday, 10:30–8:30; Closed
Wednesday.

The New York Hall of Science
The New York Hall of Science has
recently completed their 13-million
dollar expansion which features huge
new areas for high-tech exhibits, a
glass rotunda, a 300-seat auditorium
with state-of-the art-equipment, a
dining pavilion and gift shop. The
New York Hall of Science is one of
the finest inter-active hands-on science museums in the U.S.A. The perfect place to combine fun and education in a single visit.

Appendix C:

Tips for Museum-Goers

Remember, there is no formula, no right or wrong way to visit a museum, but here are some ideas that will help make your experience easy and pleasant.

1. Call before you go to make sure that the museum you want to visit is open. Hours and days of operation can change without notice.

2. Always get a museum floorplan before you start your tour. Take a few minutes to review the floorplan and decide which departments interest you most. Make checkmarks in those areas to help guide you directly to a specific location.

3. Ask questions at the information desk. Staffers are trained to give advice on what to see, where to find specific exhibits, locations of restrooms, where current special exhibitions are being shown, and which areas of the museum may be closed to visitors..

4. Wear comfortable shoes. Walking through endless galleries can be exhausting.

5. Pace yourself, especially in large museums. Take time to sit awhile, have a cup of coffee in the museum restaurant, step outside for a breath of air or browse through the museum shop.

6. If you are just browsing through galleries, let your eyes draw you into a work. You can come upon many unexpected surprises this way, and greatly increase the pleasure of your visit.

7. If nothing appeals to you in a gallery, hurry on through. There's no point wasting energy. This rule also applies to special exhibitions. Look carefully at what appeals to you, but don't spend too much time on what doesn't. You won't remember it anyway.

8. Learn as you go. Consider taking a docent tour. And remember, you can always drop out if you lose interest or if the tour lasts too long.

9. See the highlights first, especially in a large museum. This way you can take more time to look at and fully appreciate an object.

10. If you really want to concentrate, consider going alone.

11. Take as much time as you can and really look at what appeals to you!

12. Coping with enormus crowds is always difficult, especially in large museums. Try to get there early in the day when you have more energy or try to go about an hour before closing time when crowds begin to thin out.

13. At special exhibitions, if you're stuck behind a wall of people looking at a particular display, don't try to peek over shoulders. Move on to other displays and return later when you see a gap in the crowd.

14. If you don't want to take time to visit one of the mega-museums, consider going to one devoted to a single artist (such as the Rodin or the Picasso Museums in Paris) or visiting an historic house. Each has something special to offer, it's a pleasant way to spend and hour or so without crowds, and you often have the benefit of a docent who's able to take time for questions.

15. Outdoor museums can be a lot of fun. Sculpture gardens are very popular as are botanical gardens. Many art, science and specialty museums feature outdoor displays as well.

16. Visit a museum to admire its architecture. Some museums like the Guggenheim Museum of Art or the Frick Collection in New York City, the Museum of Modern Art in San Francisco, or the Palace of Versailles in Paris are good examples. So much in these buildings is to be admired: the furnishings, chandeliers, elaborate ceilings, soaring spaces, carved doors and unusual windows to name a few.

Index

Staten Island Ferry Collection, 112, 151
Staten Island Historical Society, 99, 151
Staten Island Institute of Arts and Sciences, 111–112, 151
Statue of Liberty, 112–113, 149
Stock Exchange, New York, 123, 149
Stuart, Gilbert, 53
Studio Museum in Harlem, 113–114, 143

Television, museums of, 156. *See also specific institution*
Tenement Museum, 102, 149
Textiles, collections of, 157. *See also specific institution*
Theodore Roosevelt Birthplace National Historic Site, 134, 149
Tibetan Art, Jacques Marchais Museum of, 100–101, 151
Transit Museum, 123–124, 140
Trinity Museum, Trinity Church, 149, 168

U.S.S *Intrepid* Sea-Air-Space Museum, 118–120, 146
Ukrainian Museum, 114, 149

Van Cortlandt House, 134, 142
van Gogh, Vincent, 71
Vermeer, Jan, 58
Victoriana, collections of, 157. *See also specific institution*
Video, museums of, 156. *See also specific institution*

Wave Hill, 135, 142
Whitney Museum of American Art main location, 114–115, 145
Philip Morris branch, 116, 146
Wright, Frank Lloyd, 51
Wyckoff (Pieter Claesen) House, 135, 140

**Here's where you can find
the treasures listed on the back cover:**

A collection of 12,000 toy soldiers on parade: Forbes Magazine
    Galleries

Dinosaur eggs: The American Museum of Natural History

Masterpiece paintings by Rembrandt: The Frick Collection and
    The Metropolitan Museum of Art

Knights in armor: The Metropolitan Museum of Art

Vincent van Gogh's **Starry Night:** The Museum of Modern Art

A model of New York City with 895,000 individual buildings:
    Queens Museum of Art

George Washington's desk: City Hall Governor's Room

Tyrannosaurus rex: The American Museum of Natural History

About the Author

JoAnn Bright has a Master's degree in the History of Art, and
for the past 12 years has developed and led cultural tours for the
Committee for Art at Stanford University. She also presents slide-
illustrated programs which feature highlights found in world-famous
museums.

*JoAnn's lifelong fascination with museums meshes perfectly with her
favorite hobby, traveling. Wherever she goes, her time is happily spent
seeking out new and unique places to visit. JoAnn's next guidebook,
60-Minute Museum Visits: Washington D.C. is soon to be in print,
with more books in the works for other major cities including
Chicago, Los Angeles, London, Paris, and Rome.*